Tod
Nelson
2008

I ♡ U !
*

Strong Fathers,
Strong Daughters

Strong Fathers,
Strong Daughters

---

10 Secrets Every Father Should Know

MEG MEEKER, M.D.

BALLANTINE BOOKS NEW YORK

2007 Ballantine Books Trade Paperback Edition

Published in the United States by Ballantine Books,
an imprint of The Random House Publishing Group,
a division of Random House, Inc., New York.

BALLANTINE and colophon are registered trademarks
of Random House, Inc.

Originally published in hardcover in the United States
by Regnery Publishing, a division of Eagle Publishing,
Washington, D.C., in 2006.

This edition is published by arrangement with Regnery
Publishing, a division of Eagle Publishing.

Meeker, Margaret J.
 Strong fathers, strong daughters: 10 secrets every
father should know / Meg Meeker.
   p. cm.
 Includes bibliographical references and index.
 ISBN-978-0-345-49939-4
1. Fathers and daughters. 2. Fatherhood. I. Title.
 HQ755.85.M44 2006
 306.874'2—dc22   2006022168

Printed in the United States of America

www.ballantinebooks.com

9

This book is dedicated to all the great men in my life.

To Walt and "T," you are far more than I deserve.

*To my father, Wally, thank you for my life
and for making it what it is today.*

*To my brothers Mike and Bob, you are extraordinary men
and I love you both very much.*

Contents

Strong Fathers,
Strong Daughters

Introduction

In September 1979, my father spoke a single sentence that changed my life. I had graduated from Mt. Holyoke College earlier in the year and had been rejected from several medical schools, so I was living at home pondering Plan B. One evening, on my way upstairs, I overheard my father talking to a friend on the phone. This was unusual, for my father was not a very social man and a phone conversation with a friend was noteworthy. I stopped outside the door of his study, which was slightly ajar, and listened.

"Yes," he was saying. "They really do grow up fast, don't they? I'm excited to tell you that my daughter, Meg, will be starting medical school next fall. She's not quite sure where, though."

My head went hot. I thought I was going to pass out. What was he saying? *Medical school?* I'd just received a handful of rejections. *I'll be going to medical school next fall? How can he say that?* What does he know that I don't?

His words alone didn't change the course of my life. His tone, his inflection, and his confidence had an amazing impact as well.

My father believed something about me that I couldn't believe myself. Not only did he believe it, but he, a doctor himself, put his reputation on the line in front of his friend.

As I backed away from the door, my heart rate doubled. I felt thrilled and excited, because my father's confidence gave me hope. Going to medical school had been my dream since I was a young teenager. And sure enough, in fall 1980, I started medical school, just as my father had said. He called me routinely and asked specifics about my classes. Was I understanding gross anatomy? Was I spending enough time on histology? Did I need slides to look at just for fun? It didn't matter what my response was; he packaged them up and sent them to my apartment so that I would have something interesting to do on Friday nights, which, of course, were study nights.

Don't misunderstand. My father was not a man who needed to live his life through his children. As a matter of fact, many times he discouraged me from going into medicine because he quite accurately predicted the disaster and misery of managed care medicine. I wanted to go. Did I want to because I wanted to please him? Not really. I didn't need to do that. I wanted to go because I really wanted to be like his friend—an orthopedic surgeon. This man let me come into the operating room and watch surgery for hours at a time. That was the coolest thing I had ever seen, and I wanted to be able to do it.

What my father gave me was confidence. Since I revered him as a giant in the medical field and a giant in our home, I knew that what he believed was right. It didn't matter what he said, I still believed he was right.

And he gave me a belief in myself. He communicated to me, I don't remember exactly how, that I could do anything I wanted to do. There weren't many women in his medical school class, he said, but boy were they good. They were good, and I could be too.

My father always made sure that I knew that he loved me. He was an eccentric man, quiet, antisocial, and extremely smart. He published medical papers in different languages and kidded that only peculiar people became pathologists like himself. But he loved me. I was his daughter and that was a very important thing to be. Did he tell me often? No. He didn't talk much. So how did I know? I knew because I heard him worry about me to my mother. I watched him cry when my brother and I left home for college. He came to many of my athletic events but missed many more. But that didn't matter. I knew that he thought I was terrific at sports. (In fact, he believed me to be much better than I really was, but I didn't want to set him straight on that one.) I knew he loved me because he made our entire family go on vacations together. Most of the time I hated going, particularly when I was a teen, but he made me go anyway. He knew something I didn't. He knew that we needed time to be together. In the same camp. In the same dining room. On the same hiking trails or in the same canoes.

My dad protected me fiercely, to the point where I was almost too embarrassed to date anyone. He was a hunter and he let my boyfriends know that. They saw the moose head on the wall as they entered our house, and my dad made sure that they knew who put that head up there. He thought he was being funny; I thought he was embarrassing me. But he protected me, not from predatory boys or monsters, but from myself. I was young and too trusting of people, and he knew that long before I did.

My father wasn't a good talker, and many times he didn't listen well, either. He was sometimes distracted and aloof. We used to jog together when I was in medical school, and he would ask me the same questions repeatedly while we ran. He never heard the answers—he was always, always thinking of something else. I didn't care. I just repeated myself.

My mother listened to our problems much better than my father did, but I knew who I would ask for help if my life or health were ever threatened—my dad. He was tough, he was serious, he intensely loved his family, and the most important job he held, in his mind, was to make sure that his family was cared for. We were, in fact, very well cared for.

My father is elderly now and these days I spend more time caring for him than he for me. But I know the ropes because he showed me quite well. We no longer jog together. His scoliosis causes him to shuffle along, his spine resembling a capital C, and he still repeats questions to me, no longer because he's thinking of other things, but because his memory is sliding. He has a few remaining wisps of white hair, but his eccentricity, his antisocial bent, and his love for me remain the same. He is a good man.

Most of you out there are good men as well, but you are good men who have been derided by a culture that does not care for you, that, in terms of the family, has ridiculed your authority, denied your importance, and tried to fill you with confusion about your role. But I can tell you that fathers change lives, as my father changed mine. You are natural leaders, and your family looks to you for qualities that only fathers have. You were made a man for a reason, and your daughter is looking to you for guidance that she cannot get from her mother.

What you say in a sentence, communicate with a smile, or do with regard to family rules has infinite importance for your daughter.

I want you to see yourself through her eyes. And I don't want this just for her sake, but for yours, because if you could see yourself as she sees you, even for ten minutes, your life would never be the same. When you are a child, your parents are the center of your world. If your mother is happy, your day is good. If your father is stressed, your stomach is knotted all day long at school.

Your daughter's world is smaller than yours, not just physically, but emotionally as well. It is more fragile and tender because her character is being kneaded as bread dough on a cutting board. Every day she awakens, your hands pick her up and plop her back down on the board to begin the massage. How you knead, every single day, will change who she is.

You and I have baked and we are crusty. Life has hurt us, been gracious to us, and has almost killed us. But we have survived, not because our parents continue to love us but because we have come to need someone—a friend, a spouse, or a child—to continue to care about us. Because a person who cares about us exists, we can get up in the morning.

Your daughter gets up in the morning because you exist. You were here first and she came into being because of you. The epicenter of her tiny world is you. Friends, family members, teachers, professors, or coaches will influence her to varying degrees, but they won't knead her character. You will. Because you are her dad.

Dads, you are far more powerful than you think you are. My goal in writing this book is to show you how to use your power to improve your life with your daughter, and by doing so to make your life remarkably richer, more rewarding, and more beneficial to those you love. The concepts presented in the following pages are profoundly simple. But we all know how difficult it is to implement simple truths. We know that we should love better. Or be more patient. Or be more courageous, or diligent, or faithful. But can we?

In part, it's a matter of perspective. Loving your daughter better might seem complicated to you, but it's very simple to her.

Being a hero to your daughter sounds daunting, but actually it can be quite easy. Protecting her and teaching her about God, sex, and humility doesn't require a degree in psychology. It just means being a dad.

I have not chosen attributes of fathers to discuss randomly. I have watched and listened to your daughters for many years and have heard what they say about you. I have talked to countless fathers. I have treated daughters and counseled families. I have read psychiatry texts, research papers, psychology journals, religious studies, and pediatric journals. Doing this has been my job. But I will tell you that no research paper, no textbook diagnosis, no instructions can begin to change a young girl's life as dramatically as even a handful of interactions with her father. Nothing.

From your daughter's perspective, it is never too late to strengthen her relationship with you. So be bold. Your daughter wants your guidance and support; she wants and needs a strong bond with you. And, as all successful fathers know, you need a strong bond with her. This book will show how to strengthen that bond, or rebuild it, and use it to shape your daughter's life—and yours—for the better.

Chapter One

❖

You Are the Most Important Man in Her Life

Men, good men: We need you. We—mothers, daughters, and sisters—need your help to raise healthy young women. We need every ounce of masculine courage and wit you own, because fathers, more than anyone else, set the course for a daughter's life.

Your daughter needs the best of who you are: your strength, your courage, your intelligence, and your fearlessness. She needs your empathy, assertiveness, and self-confidence. She needs *you*.

Our daughters need the support that only fathers can provide—and if you are willing to guide your daughter, to stand between her and a toxic culture, to take her to a healthier place, your rewards will be unmatched. You will experience the love and adoration that can come only from a daughter. You will feel a pride, satisfaction, and joy that you can know nowhere else.

After more than twenty years of listening to daughters—and doling out antibiotics, antidepressants, and stimulants to girls who have gone without a father's love—I know just how important fathers are. I have listened hour after hour to young girls describe how they vomit in junior high bathrooms to keep their weight down. I have listened to fourteen-year-old girls tell me they have to provide fellatio—which disgusts them—in order to keep their boyfriends. I've watched girls drop off varsity tennis teams, flunk out of school, and carve initials or tattoo cult figures onto their bodies—all to see if their dads will notice.

And I have watched daughters talk to fathers. When you come in the room, they change. Everything about them changes: their eyes, their mouths, their gestures, their body language. Daughters are never lukewarm in the presence of their fathers. They might take their mothers for granted, but not you. They light up—or they cry. They watch you intensely. They hang on your words. They hope for your attention, and they wait for it in frustration—or in despair. They need a gesture of approval, a nod of encouragement, or even simple eye contact to let them know you care and are willing to help.

When she's in your company, your daughter tries harder to excel. When you teach her, she learns more rapidly. When you guide her, she gains confidence. If you fully understood just how profoundly you can influence your daughter's life, you would be terrified, overwhelmed, or both. Boyfriends, brothers, even husbands can't shape her character the way you do. You will influence her entire life because she gives you an authority she gives no other man.

Many fathers (particularly of teen girls) assume they have little influence over their daughters—certainly less influence than their daughters' peers or pop culture—and think their daughters need to figure out life on their own. But your daughter faces a world markedly different from the one you did growing up: it's less friendly, morally unmoored, and even outright dangerous. After age six, "little girl" clothes are hard to find. Many outfits are cut to make her look like a seductive thirteen- or fourteen-year-old girl trying to attract older boys. She will enter puberty earlier than girls did a generation or two ago (and boys will be watching as she grows breasts even as young as age nine). She will see sexual innuendo or scenes of overt sexual behavior in magazines or on television before she is ten years old, whether you approve or not. She will learn about HIV and AIDS in elementary school and will also probably learn why and how it is transmitted.

When my son was in the fourth grade at a small parochial school, the teacher gave his class a science assignment. Each student was to write a report on any one of the infectious diseases from a list she gave them. My son chose to write about HIV and AIDS. (This was a popular choice because it is so widely talked about.) He learned about the virus and about drug injections and medications used to battle it. After I picked him up at school, we stopped by the grocery store. As I pulled into the parking lot, he was telling me about his findings. Then he said, "Mom, I just don't get it. I know HIV is really dangerous and that people who get AIDS die. And I get, you know, how men and women give it to each other, but what's this stuff about men giving it to other men? I just don't see how that can happen."

I took a deep breath. Now, I am not a squeamish person. I am a doctor. I'm used to talking to patients about sex-related health risks. And I believe strongly in treating all patients the same, whether they are heterosexual or homosexual. But here's what grieved me: I know from child psychology that it was too soon to detail specific sexual acts (beyond simple intercourse) to my son. It was one thing to teach him how children are conceived. It was quite another to talk about sexual acts that he cannot understand and should not be confronted with at his age. I felt as though his right to innocence had been invaded. I never withhold information, because knowledge is important, but timing is crucial.

Shocking young children breaks their healthy sense of modesty. That modesty serves a protective function. There, in the grocery store parking lot, I spoke as gently as I could, but my son was rightly upset. This knowledge and the mental pictures it drew for him taught him something he didn't want to know, and was not and could not be prepared to know at his age. In today's world, we adults do a terrible job of letting kids be kids. Our children are forced prematurely into an adult world that even our own parents or grandparents might have considered pornographic.

When your daughter hits fifth or sixth grade, she will learn what oral sex is. Before too long, she will have a pretty decent chance of seeing someone engaged in it, as the new trend in sexual behavior among adolescents is public display. She will feel comfortable saying the word *condom* and will know what they look like because she has either seen them on television or at school. Many well-meaning teachers will pride themselves on speaking openly and honestly to her about sex, determined to break the taboo about adults talking to kids about sexual activity. The problem is, many health (sex) educators are woefully behind in the information they use—and this isn't their fault. Their materials are often outdated. And many celebrities don't help. Sharon Stone, for instance, recently remarked to the teens of our nation that they should participate in oral sex rather than intercourse because, I guess, she believes it to be safer. Does she understand that *any* sexually transmitted disease (STD) a kid can get from intercourse, she/he can get from oral sex? I doubt it. Sure, she probably felt that she was on the cutting edge of the new era of sex education, but the problem is, her assumptions are outdated and she hasn't taken the time to learn the scientific facts. She doesn't see what we doctors see. Yet she and celebrities like her reach millions of teens with their various messages of "safe sex," which unfortunately aren't safe.

Teachers in most schools are no better informed. They know that a high proportion of kids are sexually active, and that many parents don't know what their kids are up to. But the teachers rely on government-mandated curricula, and government bureaucracies move slower than our knowledge about medicine. Moreover, the government's standards are not based entirely on science but on principles that many parents might not share.

Sex education curricula generally follow the guidelines of the Sexuality Information and Education Council of the United States. SIECUS is a nonprofit advocacy group that proposes to "assist children in understanding a positive view of sexuality, provide them with information and skills about taking care of their sexual health, and help them acquire skills to make decisions now and in the future." Let's review just a few of the guidelines written in the manual so that you can make your own decision about what your daughter is learning at school.

For children ages five to eight (kindergarten through second grade):

◈ Touching and rubbing one's own genitals to feel good is called masturbation.
◈ Some men and women are homosexual, which means that they will be attracted to and fall in love with someone of the same sex. (This is in the manual for the older children.)

For children ages nine to twelve (third through sixth grade):

◈ Masturbation is often the first way a person experiences sexual pleasure.
◈ Being sexual with another person usually involves more than sexual intercourse.

❖ Abortion is legal in the United States up to a certain point in pregnancy.

❖ Homosexual love relationships can be as fulfilling as heterosexual relationships. (This is in the manual for the older children.)

For children ages twelve to fifteen (seventh through tenth grade):

❖ Masturbation, either alone or with a partner, is one way people can enjoy and express their sexuality without risking pregnancy or STDs/HIV.

❖ Being sexual with another person usually involves different sexual behaviors.

❖ Having a legal abortion rarely interferes with a woman's ability to become pregnant or give birth in the future.

❖ People of all genders and sexual orientation can experience sexual dysfunction.

❖ Some sexual behaviors shared by partners include kissing, touching, caressing, massaging, and oral, vaginal, or anal intercourse.

❖ Nonprescription methods of contraception include male and female condoms, foam, gels, and suppositories.

❖ Young people can buy nonprescription contraceptives in a pharmacy, grocery store, market, or convenience store.

❖ In most states, young people can get prescriptions for contraception without their parents' permission.

❖ Both men and women can give and receive sexual pleasure.

For children ages fifteen to eighteen (tenth through twelfth grade):

 ⊕ Some sexual behaviors shared by partners include kissing, touching, talking, caressing, massaging, sharing erotic literature or art, bathing or showering together, and oral, vaginal, or anal intercourse.
 ⊕ Some people use erotic photographs, movies, or literature to enhance sexual fantasies when alone or with a partner.
 ⊕ Some sexual fantasies involve mysterious or forbidden things.
 ⊕ People can find creative and sensual ways to integrate contraception into their sexual relationship.[1]

Now let me be very clear here. I don't care what adults do regarding their sexual behaviors. But I'm a kid advocate and these guidelines bother me, as I hope they do you. First, they are scientifically illiterate. Kids can and do get STDs through mutual masturbation and oral sex. Herpes and human papillomavirus (HPV), for example, are transmitted through touch. Second, these guidelines normalize the bizarre. Sexual fantasies with mysterious things? Are we talking porn-shop stuff here? Third, they lead kids. Note the position of the later statements, which imply that if you want to enjoy pleasure, here's how to have it. Fourth, they encourage behavior (such as anal sex) that is inherently dangerous. Fifth, whatever one thinks about controversial issues like abortion, it is misleading, to say the least, to downplay the seriousness of the procedure on not only a girl's body but also on her mind and emotions.

In elementary school your daughter will learn about drugs, the dangers of sniffing glue, why she shouldn't smoke marijuana, and how bad cigarettes are for her. She will meet her friends' mothers' boyfriends. Some will be nice and some won't be. She will be taught to let someone know—a teacher, a parent, a police officer—if an adult man touches her pubic area or breasts (even if they haven't developed yet). She will be taught why her friend Sarah has two moms, or two dads, or two moms and one dad, or no mom or dad and only grandparents or foster parents. Most of this she will learn before sixth grade, while you're at work trying to get through the day and fighting your own battles.

You drive home at the end of the day, walk into your house, and there she is. Twelve years old, chasing her nine-year-old brother, screaming because he took her iPod. Then she sees you and either stops screaming or runs away, because she doesn't want you to see her ugly behavior.

Or you come home and see her watching television. Chances are, the minute you walk into the room she will grab the channel changer and flip through numerous stations. Why? Because she doesn't want you to see what she is watching—she's afraid you will be either angry or disappointed in her. Why? Because the shows aren't *Bewitched* or *The Cosby Show*. They aren't like the shows you watched growing up. The programs on television have changed right under your nose. Studies show that the amount of sexual content increased from 67 percent in 1998 to 77 percent in 2005.[2] If you grew up in the 1960s or 1970s, the amount of sexual content was, comparatively, virtually nonexistent. We'll look at this in greater detail later, but imagine: three-fourths of the shows your little girl sees have sexual content (unless she still watches *Dora the Explorer* at age twelve, which I doubt). In addition to this, the intensity of the sexual content has gotten worse.[3] In the 1960s, sexual content was Barbara Eden showing her navel on *I Dream of Jeannie*. By the 1980s, prime-time television was up to heavy kissing or allusions to petting. But that's become boring. Now, prime time offers numerous allusions to intercourse and oral sex.

For young kids—particularly early preadolescents—such sexualized images and talk can be nothing short of traumatizing.

Remember, your daughter will most likely begin puberty before her male friends. This means that from about the third grade on, you need to be very careful about what she's exposed to. While you and I might not even notice a scene of two people heading beneath the sheets, you can be sure that it raises all sorts of questions in her mind. She is forming her impressions about sex and about how teens and adults behave. If she is forced to form these impressions too young, more often than not, they will be overwhelmingly negative.

❖❖❖

When Anna was ten and halfway through her fourth-grade year, her mother brought her in for her annual physical. She was an excellent student, played soccer, and was very well adjusted. Her mother said, however, that she had recently been acting very antagonistic toward her dad. Her mother had no clue why. Anna's father had had long talks with her and went out of his way to be kind and attentive. This didn't help. Neither her mother nor I could figure out what was going on. Anna just shrugged her shoulders when I asked why she was so angry with her dad. Perhaps she was just having early pubertal "rebellion," her mother and I concluded. (Be careful when you hear this term, because nine out of ten times, this isn't normal. More is brewing beneath the surface of her behavior.)

Two more months went by, and Anna and her mother reappeared in my office. Things had gotten worse at home. Anna didn't want anything to do with her father, and her mother felt crazy. Was she missing something? Was he abusing her? The very thought made her feel guilty and nauseated. But she was so worried about Anna's behavior that even such terrible possibilities had passed through her mind. After the three of us chatted, I spoke with Anna alone. We retraced recent events in her life to try to pinpoint when the anger had started. School was okay. She had gotten along fine with her dad and brother. She hadn't gotten into a tangle with anyone at school. I gently probed for evidence of physical or sexual abuse from anyone. Nope, she said. I believed her. Finally she fell forward and her head dropped level with her shoulders. "I saw this show," she started. My ears perked up. "Well, I didn't want my parents to know because they would've been really mad at me."

"Anna, what kind of show was it?" I asked.

"I don't know the name of it or anything. I was just waiting for dinner. I had finished my homework and Mom said that I could watch TV, so I did. While I was flipping through the channels, I just saw this stuff happening. I knew I shouldn't watch, but I just kind of couldn't help it." She stopped, hoping that I would allow her to stop there. Clearly she was upset. She felt guilty, angry, and sick.

I waited. She wasn't going to talk, so I did. "Anna, who were the people in the show?"

"I don't know, just this guy and this lady. Yuck. She was kinda, you know, like, naked."

"I see. What were they doing?"

"Uh. Um. I'm not really sure, but I didn't like it at all. She had really big boobs showing and this guy was on top of her. But, see, I know all about that stuff 'cause my mom's told me. But, it was just so weird. I mean, this guy ripped her shirt and he had her pinned down. She wanted to get up and he wouldn't let her. He was really strong-looking and he was holding her hands down really tight."

"Anna, I'm so sorry you saw that. That must have made you really upset."

"I dunno. I guess so. I mean, it's just a show and all. You're not gonna tell my mom and dad, are you? They wouldn't let me watch TV for a long time."

I changed the subject, knowing that her parents had to know if they were going to help her. "Anna, why did you get so mad at your dad? Does this have anything to do with the show?" I knew, but I wanted her to see the connection.

"Well. I guess I never really thought of it that way. I mean, I know my mom and dad had to have sex once—you know, to have me. Do you think that my dad was like that to my mom? I was just thinking that she had to put up with him being mean and stuff and if she did, it would be my fault. Because if they didn't have me, then my dad wouldn't have been mean to my mom. Do you think he hurts her like that?" She looked terribly worried.

"No, absolutely not. Your dad would never do anything like that to your mom. Honey, that's not normal. That's television. Sex is really wonderful and is nothing like that at all. I'm sure that your dad would never in a million years hurt anyone that way." I had to repeat myself to help her believe me.

Anna was having a tough time, but think about her poor dad. For the last two months, in her mind, he had been a sex-crazed, woman-abusing rapist. And he didn't have a clue what was going on. Does television have an effect on your little girl? You bet it does. But you hold all the power.

❖ ❖ ❖

Perhaps you come home and notice that she is in her room. You're exhausted, and even though you assume that she is watching shows you don't approve of, you feel relieved that she is home and safe, and you're just too tired to intervene. (A word of advice to make your life easier: don't let your daughter have a TV, or a computer, in her room. Save TV time for family time when you or your wife can decide what to watch.)

You're tired a lot. If you're reading this, you are a motivated, sensitive, and caring father. You are a good man, but you're probably exhausted. For you, there is great news and bad news.

The great news is that in order to experience a richer life and raise a fabulous daughter, you don't need to change your character. You need only to indulge what's best in your character. You have everything you need for a better relationship with your daughter. You don't need to "find your feminine side," or stop watching football or drinking beer, or talk about the details of sex, birth control, and condoms with your daughter. Sure, your daughter needs your guidance, attention, and instruction, but talking to her about the serious issues of life is easier than you think.

Here's the bad news. You need to stop in your tracks, open your eyes wider, and see what your daughter faces today, tomorrow, and in ten years. It's tough and it's frightening, but this is the way it is. While you want the world to be cautious and gentle with her, it is cruel beyond imagination—even before she is a teen. Even though she may not participate in ugly stuff, it's all around her: sexual promiscuity, alcohol abuse, foul language, illegal drugs, and predatory boys and men who want only to take something from her.

I don't care whether you're a dentist, a truck driver, a CEO, or a schoolteacher; whether you live in a 10,000-square-foot home in rural Connecticut or a 1,000-square-foot apartment in Pittsburgh—ugliness is everywhere. Once upon a time ugliness was somewhat "contained"—gangs, drug pushers, and "the bad crowd" stayed in defined pockets, in certain neighborhoods and schools. No more. The ugliness is all around.

Believe it or not, I'm not a doom-and-gloom doctor. I always hope that kids have dodged the ugliness or have been "tough enough" to buck the bad stuff. Many times—especially over the last ten years—I've had a beautiful thirteen- or fourteen-year-old girl in my office and wondered whether I should ask her about sexual activity. I don't want to. I know that if I find out she is having sex, my heart will sink. She is too young. The risks are too high.

Finally the wiser, clinical physician part of my brain wins. I ask, "Are your friends sexually active?" (That's the easiest way to find out if she is.) "Do you have a boyfriend?" "What about sex—have you thought about it? Done it?" Here is where the tricky part comes in. "Sex" to kids means sexual intercourse. So I can't leave it at that. Sadly, I have to ask very specific questions about her sexual behavior.

Here is my point. Over the last ten years I've had hundreds of these interactions, and I can't tell you how many times a "good kid" looks down at the ground and nods.

As sad as this is, it makes sense, and we will go into detail as to why in a later chapter. But, fathers, you need to know that your daughters are growing up in a culture that is yanking the best right out of them. Am I exaggerating about the world your daughters face? You decide. Let's look at some national data about girls, and some about boys as well.

Sexual Activity

- ⊕ One in five Americans over age twelve tests positive for genital herpes.[4]
- ⊕ Herpes type 2 infections increased 500 percent during the 1980s.[5]
- ⊕ 11.9 percent of females will experience forced intercourse.[6]

- 40.9 percent of girls fourteen to seventeen years old experience unwanted sex, primarily because they fear that their boyfriends will get angry.[7]
- If a teen girl has had four sexual partners, and her boyfriend has had four partners, and the two have sex, she is exposed to fifteen sexual partners.[8]
- If the above number increases to eight partners each (not unusual, particularly in college), your daughter is exposed to 255 partners.[9]
- 46.7 percent of students (girls and boys) will be sexually active before high school ends.[10]
- There are five to six million new cases of human papillomavirus (HPV) infections annually.[11]
- HPV is spread through sexual contact. Some HPV strains cause cancer, some don't. HPV is responsible for approximately 99 percent of all cervical cancer cases in women.[12]
- A teen girl is at greater risk for dangerous sexually transmitted diseases because the skin overlying her cervix (epithelium) is immature. While she is a young teen, her cervix is covered with a layer called columnar epithelium. As she matures into her twenties, this is replaced with squamous epithelium, which is more resistant to viruses and bacteria.
- If a girl takes oral contraceptives for more than five years, she is four times more likely to develop cervical cancer.[13] This is most likely due to an increased number of partners and poor condom use.
- As many as 90 percent of people infected with herpes type 2 do not know they are infected.[14]
- Forty-five million people in America are infected with herpes type 2, and one million become infected each year.[15]

Depression

⊕ 35.5 percent of all high school girls have had sad, hopeless feelings for longer than two weeks. Many physicians call this clinical depression. 12.4 percent of African American females, 18.6 percent of Caucasian females, and 20.7 percent of Hispanic females have made suicide plans in the last year.[16]

⊕ Engaging in sex puts girls at higher risk for depression.[17]

⊕ 11.5 percent of females in high school attempted suicide last year.[18]

Alcohol

⊕ 27.8 percent of high school students (female and male) drank alcohol before age thirteen.[19]

⊕ Within the last year, 74.9 percent of high school students (female and male) have had one or more drinks each day for several days in a row.[20]

⊕ Within the last month, 44.6 percent of high school girls have had one or more drinks per day.[21]

⊕ 28.3 percent of high school students (female and male) had more than five drinks in a row on more than one day in the last month.[22]

Drugs

⊕ 8.7 percent of high school students have used cocaine in various forms.[23]

⊕ 12.1 percent of high school students have used inhalants one or more times.[24]

Media Use
(TV, computers, DVD, video games, music)

⊕ Kids spend, on average, 6.5 hours per day with media.[25]

⊕ 26 percent of the time, they are using more than one device.[26] This means that 8.5 hours' worth of media exposure per day is packed into 6.5 hours. (This is equivalent to a full-time job.)

⊕ Kids spend more than three hours a day watching TV.[27]

⊕ They read an average of forty-five minutes a day.[28]

⊕ Kids with TVs in their bedrooms watch, on average, an hour and a half more TV per day than kids who don't have TVs in their bedrooms.[29]

⊕ 55 percent of homes get premium cable channels like HBO.[30]

⊕ HBO and Showtime had 85 percent (the highest amount) of violent programming.[31]

The disturbing data goes on and on, but some trends do appear to be reversing. Many schools have anti-gang programs, as well as programs that discourage underage drinking and programs against smoking or taking illegal drugs. The number of teen pregnancies—and the rate of teen sexual activity—might be declining. But whatever hints of progress we might have, they're not nearly enough. Your daughter is still at terrible risk—and fathers are what stand between daughters and this toxic world.

Don't think you can't fight her "peers" or the power of pop culture. Exactly the opposite is true. Yes, the four Ms—MTV, music, movies, and magazines—are enormous influences that shape what girls think about themselves, what clothes they wear, and even the grades they get. But their influence doesn't come close to the influence of a father. A lot of research has been done on this—and fathers always come out on top. The effects of loving, caring fathers on their daughters' lives can be measured in girls of all ages.

Young Girls

- Toddlers securely attached to fathers are better at solving problems.[32]
- Six-month-old babies score higher on tests of mental development if their dads are involved in their lives.[33]
- With dads present in the home, kids manage school stress better.[34]
- Girls whose fathers provide warmth and control achieve higher academic success.[35]
- Girls who are close to their fathers exhibit less anxiety and withdrawn behaviors.[36]

Older Girls

- Parent connectedness is the number-one factor in preventing girls from engaging in premarital sex and indulging in drugs and alcohol.[37]
- Girls with doting fathers are more assertive.[38]
- Daughters who perceive that their fathers care a lot about them, who feel connected to their fathers, have significantly fewer suicide attempts and fewer instances of body dissatisfaction, depression, low self-esteem, substance use, and unhealthy weight.[39]
- Girls with involved fathers are twice as likely to stay in school.[40]
- A daughter's self-esteem is best predicted by her father's physical affection.[41]

- Girls with a father figure feel more protected, have higher self-esteem, are more likely to attempt college, and are less likely to drop out of college.[42]
- Girls with fathers who are involved in their lives have higher quantitative and verbal skills and higher intellectual functioning.[43]
- 21 percent of twelve- to fifteen-year-olds said that their number-one concern was not having enough time with their parents. 8 percent of parents said their number-one concern was not having enough time with their kids.[44]
- Girls whose parents divorce or separate before they turn twenty-one tend to have shorter life spans by four years.[45]
- Girls with good fathers are less likely to flaunt themselves to seek male attention.[46]
- Fathers help daughters become more competent, more achievement-oriented, and more successful.[47]
- Girls defer sexual activity if their parents disapprove of it, and they are less likely to be sexually active if their parents disapprove of birth control.[48]
- Girls with involved fathers wait longer to initiate sex and have lower rates of teen pregnancy. Teen girls who live with both parents are three times less likely to lose their virginity before their sixteenth birthdays.[49]
- 76 percent of teen girls said that fathers influenced their decisions on whether they should become sexually active.[50]
- 97 percent of girls who said they could talk to their parents had lower teen pregnancy rates.[51]
- 93 percent of teen girls who had a loving parent had a lower risk of pregnancy.[52]
- A daughter from a middle-class family has a fivefold lower risk of out-of-wedlock pregnancy if her father lives at home.[53]

⊕ Girls who lived with their mothers and fathers (as opposed to mothers only) have significantly fewer growth and developmental delays, and fewer learning disorders, emotional disabilities, and behavior problems.[54]

⊕ Girls who live with their mothers only have significantly less ability to control impulses, delay gratification, and have a weaker sense of conscience or right and wrong.[55]

⊕ When a father is involved in his kids' day-to-day activities, they are more likely to confide in him and seek his emotional support.[56]

⊕ Parental control and monitoring are effective deterrents against adolescent misbehavior.[57]

⊕ Kids do better academically if their fathers establish rules and exhibit affection.[58]

Your daughter takes cues from you, her father, on everything from drug use, drinking, delinquency, smoking, and having sex, to self-esteem, moodiness, and seeking attention from teen boys.

When you are with her, whether you eat dinner and do homework together or even when you are present but don't say much, the quality and stability of her life—and, you'll find, your own—improves immeasurably. Even if you think the two of you operate on different planes, even if you worry that time spent with her shows no measurable results, even if you doubt you are having a meaningful impact on her, the clinical fact is that you are giving your daughter the greatest of gifts. And you're helping yourself too—research shows that parenting may increase a man's emotional growth and increase his feelings of value and significance.[59]

Your daughter will view this time spent with you vastly differently than you do. Over the years, in erratic bursts and in simple ordinary life together, she will absorb your influence. She will watch every move you make. She might not understand why you are happy or angry, dishonest or affectionate, but you will be the most important man in her life, forever.

When she is twenty-five, she will mentally size her boyfriend or husband up against you. When she is thirty-five, the number of children she has will be affected by her life with you. The clothes she wears will reflect something about you. Even when she is seventy-five, how she faces her future will depend on some distant memory of time you spent together. Be it good or painful, the hours and years you spend with her—or don't spend with her— change who she is.

❖ ❖ ❖

At age eighteen, Ainsley left her small Midwestern hometown and began life at an Ivy League college. She enjoyed her first year, but during her second year something shifted inside her. Now, at age fifty-one, she still can't explain why she changed that year.

During her sophomore year, Ainsley began acting wild. She drank too much, and was eventually kicked out of school. She had to call her mother and father to tell them that she was returning home. She packed up her posters, books, and disappointment, and drove home alone.

Ainsley spent the next twenty-four hours behind the wheel of her Jeep, frightened, relieved, and anxious. What would her parents say? Would they cry, scream, or both? In the midst of her wondering, something felt peculiarly good. She didn't know how or why, but she wanted her parents to help her figure out life for the next six months.

When she finally parked in the driveway of her parents' house, she saw her dad's Chevy in the garage. No one met her outside.

She walked up the steps and peered like a stranger through the window to see them before they saw her. They were drinking coffee in the kitchen. Somehow this made her feel more in charge.

The door was unlocked. Ainsley said that the next few minutes changed her life forever. As she pushed the door open, she saw her mother first, her face puffy and red from crying. She looked tired, angry, and sad. Ainsley went to her and hugged her.

Then she saw the look on her father's face. Anticipating anger and disappointment, she was confused by his expression. He looked strangely calm and kind. She hugged him and wanted to cry but she couldn't.

Her mother shouted that Ainsley had been foolish. She had thrown away her future. She had shamed their family. Ainsley stood quietly and listened. Then, in the middle of her mother's lecture, her father came toward her and whispered, "Are you all right?" She burst into tears.

Ainsley realized at that moment that her father knew her better than she knew herself. While she felt confused, she understood that he saw right through her; he recognized, as no one else could, that something was broken inside the girl he cherished. Ainsley's father didn't make her work the night shift at McDonald's or at the local gas station. He waited, he listened, and he kept his hurt to himself. He wasn't concerned with what family and friends would think. He didn't worry about how the expulsion would change her future. He was worried about her.

"You can't imagine how that felt," Ainsley told me. "It was over thirty years ago. The love I felt from him is as fresh and new as it was then. I knew he loved me. Sure, he was proud of me, but that was always on the periphery of our relationship. He didn't let his disappointment or anger ever supersede his love. In those moments after I walked through the door, I got a glimpse of who I was in his eyes. I knew then that I, not what I accomplished, was what he cherished." She stopped abruptly and her nose and cheeks turned red. She smiled through a few plump tears and shook her head, still marveling in disbelief at the man she loved and missed so dearly. Her father made the difference in her life. You will make the difference in your daughter's life.

You have to—because, unfortunately, we have a popular culture that's not healthy for girls and young women, and there is only one thing that stands between it and your daughter. You.

Fathers inevitably change the course of their daughters' lives—and can even save them. From the moment you set eyes on her wet-from-the-womb body until she leaves your home, the clock starts ticking. It's the clock that times your hours with her, your opportunities to influence her, to shape her character, and to help her find herself—and to enjoy living. In the chapters that follow, we'll look at how fathers can help their daughters: physically, emotionally, intellectually, and spiritually.

Chapter Two

✣

She Needs a Hero

"What are you going to be when you grow up?" You probably started hearing that when you were eight years old. Chances are, your first thoughts were about Superman, or you wanted to be a cowboy, a fireman, a knight, or a football star. What you really wanted to be was a hero.

Well, I have news for you. Your daughter wants a hero—and she has chosen you.

Think about heroes: they protect people, they persevere, they exhibit altruistic love, they are faithful to their inner convictions, and they understand right from wrong and act on it. No fireman counts the odds when he runs through sheets of flame and showers of concrete to save just one terrified person.

Heroes are humble, but to those they rescue, they are bigger than life.

So how do you become a hero to your daughter? First, you should know that she can't survive without one. She needs a hero to navigate her through a treacherous popular culture. And you should know that being a twenty-first-century hero is tough stuff. It requires emotional fortitude, mental self-control, and physical restraint. It means walking into embarrassing, uncomfortable, or even life-threatening situations in order to rescue your daughter.

You might need to show up at a party where your daughter's friends—and maybe your daughter—have been drinking, and take her home. You might need to talk to her about the clothes she wears and the music she likes. And yes, you might even need to get in the car at one in the morning, go to her boyfriend's house, and insist that she come home.

Here's what your daughter needs from you.

Leadership

When your daughter is born, she recognizes your voice as deeper than her mother's. As a toddler, she looks up at your enormous frame and realizes that you are big, smart, and tough. In her grade school years, she instinctively turns to you for direction.

Whatever outward impression she gives, her life is centered on discovering what you like in her, and what you want from her. She knows you are smarter than she is. She gives you authority because she needs you to love and adore her. She can't feel good about herself until she knows that you feel good about her. So you need to use your authority carefully and wisely. Your daughter doesn't want to see you as an equal. She wants you to be her hero, someone who is wiser and steadier and stronger than she is.

The only way you will alienate your daughter in the long term is by losing her respect, failing to lead, or failing to protect her. If you don't provide for her needs, she will find someone else who will—and that's when trouble starts. Don't let that happen.

Nowadays, the idea of assuming authority makes many men uneasy. It smacks of political incorrectness. Pop psychologists and educators have told us that authority is suffocating, obtrusive, and will crush a child's spirit. Fathers worry that if they push their kids or establish too many rules, they'll just rebel. But the greatest danger comes from fathers who surrender leadership, particularly during their children's teen years. Authority is not a threat to your relationship with your daughter—it is what will bring you closer to your daughter, and what will make her respect you more.

In fact, girls who end up in counselors' offices, detention centers, or halfway homes are not girls who had authoritative fathers. Quite the opposite. Troubled young women spend most of their time in counseling describing the hurt they felt from fathers who abandoned them, retreated from their lives, or ignored them. They describe fathers who failed—or were afraid—to establish rules. They describe fathers who focused on their own emotional struggles rather than those of their daughters. They describe fathers who wanted to avoid any conflict and so shied away from engaging their daughters in conversation or challenging them when they made bad decisions.

Your natural instinct is to protect your daughter. Forget what pop culture and pop psychologists tell you. Do it.

And be ready. Your daughter wants you to be an authority figure, but as she matures, she will likely test you to see if you're serious. Dads, as a rule, know adolescent boys will eventually start to challenge them. The one-on-one basketball games will get more competitive, and the son will start to buck dad's authority.

Let me tell you a secret: many daughters challenge their fathers too. They'll dive into a power struggle with you, not to see how tough you are, but to see how much you really care about them.

So remember that when she pushes hard against your rules, flailing, crying that you are mean or unfair, she is really asking you a question: Am I worth the fight, Dad? Are you strong enough to handle me? Make sure she knows the answer is yes.

When I was in college, my father was so protective I thought that he was a borderline psychotic. I attended an all-women's college (my own decision) and really didn't give my parents much trouble. I was the oldest girl in the family and had a firstborn's sense of responsibility. One summer night before my senior year, a handsome fellow who had recently graduated from college and held a very respectable job invited me to dinner. When he came to my house to pick me up, my dad introduced himself. Unfortunately (or fortunately) for me, something about the fellow rubbed my dad the wrong way. I couldn't see it because, quite honestly, the guy was really cute. My father asked what time I would be home. Yes, he reminded me, I was living at his home for the summer and that included a curfew. I told him that I would be home at midnight.

We went to a fancy restaurant and afterward went to another for dessert and drinks (the drinking age was eighteen back then). Needless to say, I was so enamored with my date that I forgot about the time. It was 12:30 a.m. All of a sudden, at this lovely, quiet restaurant, I heard my name called over the PA system, telling me that I had a phone call. I was mortified. I knew exactly who was calling. I was so embarrassed that I simply asked my date to drive me home. I was furious with my father. He was waiting at the front door with the porch lights on. My date walked me into the house. The poor guy needed to use the restroom, but before he could get there, my father told him he didn't care for the way he had kept me out so late, especially when he had known I was supposed to be home an hour earlier. Then he actually told the poor guy that he was no longer welcome in our home, because he had been disrespectful to me! My date was so upset he left without using the bathroom.

I was seeing red, poised to verbally duke it out with my dad. I was twenty years old, I told him, and fully capable of deciding when I should be home. I refused to be treated like an out-of-control adolescent girl. I yelled at him. He yelled back and let me know in no uncertain terms that I was in his home and he had every right to tell me when I had to be back. I didn't speak to him for two days. I wasn't as upset about the rules as I was embarrassed by being called at the restaurant and, worse, to have my date kicked out of the house!

I went on a few more dates with the man (he never came back to the house; I met him out) and really thought he was wonderful. He was gracious, intelligent, and fun to be with. Also, he was very polite and, whatever my dad said, I thought he treated me with respect, and I liked that. One day, I dropped by his house unannounced. I felt very relaxed with him, and just felt like saying hello. When I knocked on the door, I was greeted by a gorgeous twenty-something blonde. I felt sick. Particularly when I found out that the skunk wasn't entertaining just her, but other women as well.

I realized then that my dad recognized in this man something that I hadn't. The tough guy back home, who insisted on curfews even when I was a grown-up and who told me exactly what he thought about the men I dated, was right, as he'd been right many times before. He never once reneged on the authority he felt as my father—and I can tell you now that nothing feels better to a teen or young daughter than being protectively embraced by Dad's strong arms. His authority kept me out of trouble, it made me feel loved, and more than anything, it made me proud that he was my dad.

Your daughter needs your guideposts of right and wrong, of proper and improper behavior. When she hits third grade or high school or marriage—all new experiences for her—she needs to know what you think is best for her. You've been there before. She trusts your opinion. So let her know. Don't be afraid. And don't shy away from the big questions in life. She'll want to know what you think her life's purpose is: whether you believe she should indulge her own passions or devote herself to helping others.

❖ ❖ ❖

When Ellie was fifteen years old, she came to me for a checkup. She was excited, and after a few minutes of chatting she told me why.

"My dad and I just got back from Peru," she blurted. "It was so cool. You can't believe how beautiful the mountains were and how amazing the people were we met."

"How nice, Ellie. Who all went on your trip?"

"Just my dad and me."

"What about your mother, your brother and sister? Didn't they want to go on vacation with you?"

"Oh no, we weren't on vacation," she said. "We went to bring medical supplies to people in the Andes who don't have any. My dad and I planned our trip a year ago and this was something he just wanted to do with me, I guess."

"That must have been fun."

"Well, I really wouldn't call it fun. It was incredibly hard. We hiked up the mountain every day starting at about ten thousand feet and set up clinics in empty rooms and sometimes outside. I took blood pressures and gave fluoride treatments to kids and grown-ups, and my dad treated their sicknesses."

I stopped my exam, picturing this elfish young girl hiking up mountains, shoving trays of fluoride paste into strangers' mouths, and sleeping outside.

"What in the world prompted your dad to take you on the trip?"

"Oh, I don't know. He has always been the kind of guy who looks out for people who are poor or sick. Even here at home since I was really little he would take me with him to the soup kitchen in town. One time I remember my mom got real mad at him because we went to pick up Chinese food for dinner. On the way home he saw a guy rummaging through a trash can at a park. He stopped the car, jumped out with all of our Chinese food, and asked the man what he would like to eat. The guy chose the egg rolls—my mom's favorite. That's why she got mad. He never told her about the guy in the park, she just thought he forgot them. So I guess going to Peru was just what's natural for him. He loves taking care of others."

"What about you?" I asked. "Did you like what you were doing in Peru?"

"Oh yeah, I loved it. It was amazing. I really wanted to go. You know, watching my dad, who's this big-shot, really smart doctor, go off to help people who don't have enough food, who die of gross stuff like worms and junk, makes me want to do it too. I know a lot of my friends' dads don't do stuff like this. But my dad's amazing. He's always thinking about what others need more than what he wants. I think that's cool and I want to be like him. That's why I went."

By living his beliefs, Ellie's father led her to the same spot.

Do a gut check on your own beliefs, and think of what sort of woman you want your daughter to be. She'll learn not only from what you say, but from what you do.

One of the best things fathers can do is raise their daughters' expectations of life. That will directly affect how your daughter talks, how she dresses, how well she does in school, even what sports or musical instruments she chooses to play. You can help her set goals, help her define a higher purpose for her life, and as a result, her self-esteem will skyrocket. And it will bring you closer, because she'll recognize you as a leader and an ally, helping her to chart a better course.

My teenage patients know that I am a strong advocate of teens postponing sexual activity. They know that I will talk to them about sex. They know what I will say. And even if they don't want to listen, they almost always respond positively because they know I'm on their side, that I care about their future.

Fathers need to be strict, but they also need to be kind, accepting, and loving. It's a matter of balance. The don'ts are easy. Don't let your daughter think of you as the enemy. Don't use your authority in ways that are cruel or that sting. Don't try to live your life through hers. Don't try to make her your robot. But do lead.

If you don't accept the authority that is naturally yours, if you don't set high standards, if you don't act to protect your daughter, if you don't live a life of moral principle, your daughter will suffer, as my patient Leah suffered.

❖ ❖ ❖

I met Leah when she was sixteen years old. When I pushed open the exam room door, I saw her sitting with her mother. They looked very solemn. They weren't reading magazines or talking or even looking at the pictures on the walls.

"Hello, Leah, I'm Dr. Meeker. It's nice to meet you." I offered my hand.

"Hi."

She didn't look up.

I waited.

She still didn't look up.

Her mother broke the awkward silence. "I'm Leah's mother, Dr. Meeker. She really doesn't want to be here. I made her come because something's wrong. I'm really worried she's depressed."

As Leah's mother spoke, I watched Leah. All I saw was the top of her head. She sat hunched over, her hands tucked in the opposite sleeves of her shirt, her legs crossed beneath her in the metal chair.

When her mother spoke, Leah didn't flinch.

"When do you feel her depression started?"

"Well... you see, Dr. Meeker, this is kind of embarrassing."

Leah looked at her mother and shook her head, trying to stop her.

"Leah, we have to talk about this. I know it's tough but it's very important."

Leah's gaze returned to the carpet.

"You see, a couple of months ago Leah went to her friend's house. He was her best friend. They had known each other since the fourth grade. Anyway, they spent a lot of time together. You know, not dating or anything. Actually, Leah was just beginning to date another guy, his name was Jeremy." Her mother paused, and Leah began to shift in her seat.

"Well, anyway, this friend—her boy 'friend,' not Jeremy—asked Leah to help him with a paper he was writing. Dr. Meeker, they studied together all the time. This particular day, I think it was a Tuesday—no, Leah, was it a Thursday?"

I was growing impatient but waited.

"Doesn't matter. She said that, yes, she would help him and they went to his house after school. Apparently—now, Leah, you correct me if I'm wrong—apparently they were sitting on the couch studying and out of the blue he pushed himself on her."

Leah's mother stopped for a moment. Leah began sobbing.

"Leah," I tried. "Is that what happened?"

Leah nodded her head. Her mother continued. "I don't know all that happened, you know, sexually. But whatever it was it really upset her."

Leah cried harder.

Over the next forty-five minutes, I learned from the tentative sixteen-year-old girl and her mother that Leah's trusted friend had suddenly "turned on her" and forced her to participate in many sexual acts.

"Leah, do you realize what this boy did to you was illegal? He should be in jail right now. What did your father do?"

She delivered her father's response in a monotone voice. "My dad said to me, 'Boys will be boys,' and left to go golfing."

❖ ❖ ❖

The assault was devastating to Leah, but the blow that had brought her down was the fact that her father didn't care and didn't defend her. He could have been Leah's hero. He could have stormed over to the young man's house and demanded an apology for his daughter; he could have demanded that the young man turn himself over to the police. But instead, he went golfing.

If her dad had done anything to defend her—even a simple angry phone call to the young man—he could have spared his daughter months of agony. Instead, it took eighteen months of counseling to help her depression abate.

It is a fundamental principle of human behavior that having an authority makes us feel good. Yes, all of us. While instinctively we want to buck it, when the sky falls in, we run to it. When confronted by any problem, any challenge, any mess that we can't get ourselves out of, we want someone who has answers, someone who can offer support, someone who can offer a helping hand and who knows what to do.

Dad, that's what your daughter wants from you. Your daughter doesn't have to like your mannerisms, your rules, your clothes, or your political views, but you never want to lose her respect. And you won't if you live your moral beliefs and act with authority. If you do that, you will be a hero in her eyes. It's what she wants you to be. And I can say, as a pediatrician: Don't back out. Please. She needs you, possibly more than you can imagine.

Many psychiatrists believe that a father's response is the most important factor in how quickly a girl recovers mentally from a sexual assault. In fact, how a father responds to his daughter's sexual assault can be as significant a turning point in her life as the assault itself. Think about this for a moment. A sexual assault is possibly the most traumatic event a girl can experience. Now consider that many psychologists and psychiatrists say *your response* to your daughter's assault is as important as the event itself to your daughter's future emotional health. This makes sense, and here's why.

When a child (or adult) is humiliated or harmed, her natural instinct is to get back at the offender, to fight, to defend herself. Every ounce of her screams to claw, to run, to do something—but she is physically weaker than her attacker. Now she sees you. In her eyes, you are big, tough, and smart. Her gut tells her, "He can help. He's the answer. My dad will make things right because he loves me. My dad will kill him. He'll stand up for me." Before you even learn what's happened, she has imagined your heroic response. Mom can't do it, but you can.

If you do what your instinct tells you to do—if you get angry and take action—she will feel affirmed. She will feel loved. She will feel defended. She will feel a sense of justice. She will feel a sense of closure over the horrible incident. When you respond as her hero, both of you win.

But if you respond as Leah's dad did, you achieve the exact opposite effect on every count. Your daughter will feel discredited, unloved, and undefended. She will feel that dad is not someone she can count on. She will feel no sense of closure, no sense of justice having been done, and she will even think that the horrible assault is what she has to expect from boys. And the result will be deep and long-lasting depression.

Leah was betrayed by her friend and failed by her father, and she suffered depression, confusion, and a sense of helplessness and anxiety that a mother's care couldn't begin to alleviate without eighteen months of counseling. Would Leah have recovered sooner if her dad had acted as a hero? I know the answer is yes because I've seen hundreds of Leahs. And I submit that if he acted as a man ought, rather than shrugging his shoulders in weakness, he might have prevented Leah's depression.

Dad, it's not optional: your daughter needs you to be her hero.

Perseverance

One of the toughest aspects of being a hero to your daughter is not just deciding what is good and right for her, but also keeping her on track. Fathers can demand tremendous discipline from themselves, but they can find it much harder to stand firm with their children. Fathers get tired. Daughters can become defiant, manipulative, and wear their fathers down. This is where perseverance comes in.

I have seen this operate in my own home. My husband and I work together. With patients he is clear and decisive and expects that his advice will be followed. Then he comes home. When our seventeen-year-old daughter insists on going to a beach party with friends until one in the morning, he listens attentively. It's ten o'clock at night and we're both exhausted. She isn't, so she looks at her dad and offers, "*Pleeease*, Dad." Then something peculiar happens. Rational convictions leap from his brain. This man who only hours before was clear and firm about what was best for his patients goes to complete mush. "Oh, honey, I guess if you promise to be home by one, you can go."

"Are you crazy?" I blurt out. "Seventeen-year-old guys and seventeen-year-old girls on a beach until one in the morning? I don't think so."

Too often fathers give in to daughters and then rationalize it away: "All kids experiment with alcohol and sex and a little bit of drugs, I can't keep her from that forever," or "Now that she's seventeen she's mature enough to handle herself." But this is the same daughter who, when she was ten years old, you pledged to protect from all these things—and the dangers aren't over. They're getting worse.

Sure, other kids are experimenting with sex and drugs and alcohol, but other kids aren't your daughter. And your daughter will respect you more if you don't give in. The minute you waffle on your convictions, you lose stature in your daughter's eyes. She thinks you're smarter than other parents, tougher than her boyfriend, and care more about her—and what's right for her—than other people. Let me tell you a secret about daughters of all ages: they love to boast about how tough their dads are—not just physically, but how strict and demanding they are. Why? Because this allows daughters to "show off" how much their fathers love them. If only you could be privy to the private conversations of girlfriends.

If you only had to fight for her once, twice, or even ten times, the process wouldn't be so tough. But you might have to fight for her two hundred times. You only have eighteen short years before she is on her own. If you don't show her the high road now, she won't find it later. Perseverance in setting her on that road isn't easy. She might appear embarrassed by your interventions. She might sulk. She might even say she hates you. But you can see what she can't. You know how sixteen-year-old boys react when they see her in a halter top. You know how even one beer can make her unsafe to drive. You know a lot more than she does, and however hard it is to persevere in leading her the right way, you have to do it.

And that means not just setting and enforcing rules, but leading by example. When you persevere, even when your principles cost you dearly, she learns the lesson. She'll see you as a hero, and if she admires what you do, she will do it too.

Now here we must face a thorny issue—divorce. It's important for every good father to know the impact of divorce on his daughter. Only then can you help her.

Volumes of research on daughters and sons consistently reveal that divorce hurts kids. That's just the way it is. Daughters often feel abandoned, guilty, sad, and angry. They often become depressed. No matter how much a father tries to convince a daughter that it wasn't her fault, it doesn't matter. Up through adolescence, young people usually see themselves at the center of their family and friends, and they feel, whatever happens, happens in large part because of them. So your daughter might not only feel responsible for your divorce, she could also feel devastated and guilty that she can't change your or her mother's mind about it.

These feelings exist regardless of what you do. Only time and maturity help her sort this out.

But your daughter will also feel abandoned. She'll ask, "What was wrong with me? Wasn't I worth sticking around for? If Mom really loved me, why did she walk out?" This is where you must begin to help her.

Your daughter expects parents to stay married. If she sees you or her mother renege on that commitment, she becomes confused. Heroes, in her mind, keep fighting. In reality, though, sometimes you can't. If Mom leaves, has an affair, or abandons the family through drinking, your fight is limited.

But whenever, for your daughter's sake, you can fight, you must. How you fight, how you persevere, how you manifest your courage will *always* influence your daughter. Sometimes perseverance for your daughter's sake means sticking with her crazy mother. Maybe it means sacrificing your own happiness for hers. This is what heroes do. It is what your daughter expects. Making the heroic choice at work, in marriage, and throughout your life will shape your daughter, who she is and what she becomes. You need to lead her wisely, consistently, heroically.

And sometimes heroism gives us second chances.

❖ ❖ ❖

Doug turned to look out his window. The whole point of vacationing in Florida was to celebrate twenty-five years of marriage with his wife, Judy, to reconnect with her, to bring something fresh to their relationship. The last thing he wanted to hear were Judy's complaints about how friends of hers had been criticizing her back home.

Suddenly, his eyes went black. He heard shrieks from tearing metal. Glass shattered, tires burned and burst. His body was thrown. His mind couldn't make sense of it. Was a bomb exploding? Was he dying or drowning?

Then came a terrible silence. Doug forced himself to be calm. His engineer's thinking took over. *Just take a few deep breaths. Figure out the problem. Face it, find a solution.* He shoved open his crushed car door.

Doug paused. He was telling me about the horrible accident that had happened more than ten years ago. His great fear, he said, was that as he shoved against the car door to escape and then rescue Judy, he heard nothing: no cries, no screams, nothing. Then he saw Judy's shoe. As he spoke, his black eyes turned away, and he cried.

Through his tears, Doug continued. The accident had happened on the Florida causeway, heading toward the Keys. An oncoming car had crossed the center line and hit Judy's side head-on. She was immediately thrust into a coma. Weeks went by as she lay in the intensive care unit of a strange hospital. Doctors told Doug that Judy would soon die. But she didn't.

While he waited, Doug asked a friend to search the remains of the rental car. He wanted to find his daily planner. He needed to restore order to his life. After all, he was an engineer.

His friend returned with the planner in hand. As Doug took it, he had an epiphany. He told me, "If God could return my day planner from the mangled steel of that car, surely he could give me back my wife."

Doug prayed. He persevered in hope that someday Judy would open her eyes, get off the hospital bed, and walk.

Then Judy did open her eyes. She fixed her gaze on Doug and the doctors. But behind her eyes, she wasn't there. She recognized no one, remembered nothing.

Doug's daughter Mindy took over the story.

"When my father brought my mother home from Florida, I was nineteen and scared. The mom I knew had died and someone else wore her clothes and stood in her shoes. She looked thin and ill. She couldn't remember the movies we had seen together, the endless nights she had helped me with homework. I was grieving and felt crazy.

"Life was really, really hard. The mother I knew was gone. My dad's wife was changed. I felt extremely protective of my little sister and I felt protective of my dad. Our relationship became quite peculiar. I took over much of my mother's role—which of course neither my dad nor I wanted—running the house and looking after my sister."

Mindy's body language was telling. She wasn't stiff or uncomfortable; she was attentive and clear. She looked directly into my eyes as she spoke. Sometimes she cried and occasionally she laughed.

Before the accident, she had deeply loved and revered her father. After the accident, her love and respect for him had soared. He became her hero.

"When he brought Mom home, she couldn't remember anything. My dad brought out photo albums and hired a teacher to help. It wasn't my dad's nature to be patient, but week after week, month after month, he worked with her. And he helped us kids, me and my younger brother and sister.

"Other fathers might not have been able to take it: to wake up every morning to a wife who didn't know you; to reteach her twenty-five years' worth of life. But my dad never gave up. Of course he knew that my mother would never be the same. He didn't know what was ahead. And that was the amazing part—he always looked forward.

"He changed his work schedule. He retired early and moved my mother up north, where life would be quieter and simpler. I know he still worries a lot about her."

"What was the greatest lesson your father taught you?" I asked.

"Undiluted faithfulness." She beamed. "He never caved. He stuck it out. He held on to God with his life and he fought for my mother."

Now, as an adult, Mindy realizes her father wasn't fighting just for Judy; he was fighting for her. He wanted Mindy to have stability. He wanted her to share his strong faith. He wanted his oldest daughter to find her own depth of strength. Was he her hero? Absolutely, Mindy told me. No one else could hold a candle to him.

❖ ❖ ❖

Doug is a hero. I'm sure he doesn't think of himself that way; heroes never do. But Doug is what a father should be. All men are capable of doing what Doug did.

You may not think so. You may think his life sounds miserable. You may even think he's a fool to have stuck it out.

But you haven't seen Doug's face as he talks. You haven't heard his calm voice imparting the wisdom he has learned from this experience. It is extraordinary. Doug has something I want, and something you want. It is an indescribable peace, a joy that comes only from persevering and doing what is right, even in the midst of anguish.

Doug is a great hero because he saved his family. That's what heroes do. They meet the deepest needs of the human heart.

This is sobering stuff and I don't take any of what I am saying lightly. It hits hard, but it is truthful, and someone has to tell fathers to uncage their masculinity. In too much of popular culture, masculinity is either disparaged (often by feminists) or displayed wrongly (as in rap music). True masculinity is the moral exercise of authority. And your little girl needs it.

Here are a few pointers that all dads should have.

1. *Make a plan.* Your aspirations for your daughter will be clearest when she is young. When she's an infant, you know with crystal clarity what you will expect from her: everything from what she will be allowed to say and do to whom she can date. Write it down now, and keep it clear in your mind and in hers. Teens love to tangle with your thinking. So have your rules inscribed like the Ten Commandments—and stick to them.

2. *Have courage under fire.* Yes, you will be fired upon—by friends, pop psychologists, television programs, your wife, and your daughter. Keep your cool, but be firm and consistent. In the best men, kindness, strength, and perseverance go together.

3. *Be the leader.* Remember that you have far more life experience than your daughter. Even if her IQ is higher than yours, she can't make decisions as well as you can. You can see the big picture and weigh the consequences of actions in a way that she can't. Young children, particularly smart young children, have an astonishingly cunning ability to manipulate fathers. So, nice men, beware. When your two-year-old daughter has a temper tantrum, put her in time-out and ignore her until she calms down. When she's sixteen, do exactly the same. If you need to ground her for a week, or a month, do it. And don't ever take personally the venom spewing from her lovely tongue. She's still a kid. So you lead;

don't let her. She'll have the entire rest of her life to run the
show when she has her own home.

4. *Don't cave, persevere.* Heroes see a battle through until the
end; they never run away. So stay in the fight, stay engaged
with your daughter and your family, spend as much time at
home as you can, stay consistent, loving, kind, and patient,
and remember that you are more resilient than your daughter is. Parents often say that kids are resilient in crises like
divorce. But they're not; kids just don't have a choice. You
do. You can make the choice not to run when things get
tough. You daughter can't tell you this, so I will: If there is
any way you can stay married, do it. Even if your marriage
seems doomed, stay in it, stay at home with your children
for as long as possible, for their sake. Getting divorced when
your daughter is twenty is better for her than when she's
fourteen. And you might find that the best remedy for a bad
marriage is sticking it out. Things really can improve.

Don't bend under peer pressure. You will have friends (probably most of your friends) who will be much more lenient with their
daughters. So what? The risks out there are very real. I see them in
my examination rooms every day, and I appreciate—and daughters and wives appreciate—fathers who are heroes, fathers who
don't relax until the battle leaves home (and really not even then).

This is a tall order, but I have seen enough heroic fathers to
know that it's an order that every good man can fill if he sets himself to it. All it requires is that you be a man, a real man, which
means a man of courage, perseverance, and integrity. You were
made a man for a reason. You were made a man to be a strong,
loving husband and father. So listen to your instincts, and do
what's right. Be a hero.

Chapter Three

❖

You Are Her First Love

Thomas Aquinas regarded love as the root of all other passions—hate, jealousy, and fear—and when I talk to daughters about their fathers, the conversations are almost always emotionally charged. They adore their fathers or hate them—sometimes they do both simultaneously. Your daughter yearns to secure your love, and throughout her life she'll need you to prove it.

A daughter identifies easily with her mother, but you are a mystery to her. You are her first love, so the early years of your relationship with her are crucial. The love you give her is her starting point. You have other loves in your life, but she doesn't. Every man who enters her life will be compared to you; every relationship she has with a man will be filtered through her relationship with you. If you have a good relationship, she will choose boyfriends who will treat her well. If she sees you as open and warm, she'll be confident with other men. If you are cold and unaffectionate, she'll find it hard to express love in a healthy way.

When your daughter was born, oxygen was forced into her lungs so she could breathe. So too must love be pressed into her being if she is to grow into an emotionally sound woman.

You will naturally feel love toward your daughter—especially in those first years of life—but that doesn't guarantee she feels loved by you. Daughters' reactions to words, actions, and situations are more complex, reflective, and diverse than those of fathers. She will read a litany of possible meanings into everything you do. When you buy your daughter a bracelet for her birthday, you'll think of it as a straightforward gift. But she will think of it as fraught with meaning, good or bad.

One of my standard questions when I'm examining a girl is "Tell me who in your life loves you." About half the girls respond, "My mom and dad, I guess. You know, they have to." A quarter of them look at me quizzically. And the remaining quarter shrug their shoulders and say, "I don't know."

My observations aren't unique. A nationwide survey by the National Commission on Children found that when asked whether their parents "really cared" about them, 97 percent of kids between the ages of ten and seventeen from intact families believed their fathers really cared. For children in stepfamilies, 71 percent said their fathers really cared. In single-parent families, the number was 55 percent.

If you're in a stable marriage, you have done your daughter an enormous favor. But with the culture the way it is, you need to be vigilant. To be certain your daughter feels loved by you, here are some practical steps you can take.

Words

Use them. One of the major differences between men and women is how they use words. Women like to talk; men don't.

That's just the way it is. You might spend three hours watching a football game with your son and never say a word—and both of you would be happy. But your daughter isn't wired like that. You have to talk to her. A good rule of thumb is to use twice as many words as you normally would, even if it means just saying things twice. Daughters can be prone to self-doubt. Pay her compliments repeatedly, so she knows you're sincere.

When she talks, she wants you to respond. Your daughter is sensitive not only to herself, but to others, and is always asking herself: Does he like being with me? Is he quiet because he's thinking about something? Is he angry? Is he depressed? She wants you to be happy because then her life is better. She'll often act as your personal aide, doing what she can to improve things. You are the center of her world.

In return, you need, first and foremost, to tell her you love her. Not just on special occasions, but regularly. That might be easy when she's five, but she needs to hear it even more when she is fifteen. She needs to hear you say it all the time. When a daughter hears "I love you" from her father, she feels complete.

But your job doesn't end there, because her next question might be: "I love you too, Dad, but why? Why do you love me?"

You might find this exasperating, but she needs to hear the words. She wants to know why you feel the way you do, to test your sincerity. Men can find this frustrating, but I'm giving you fair warning. Girls who are seven years old might be satisfied with "I love you." Girls of seventeen will want an explanation. She's not trying to push your buttons. She genuinely wants to know.

So you need to be ready. Reflect on your daughter's character, praise her best attributes, talk about her sensitivity, compassion, or courage. Your daughter will draw a picture in her mind of how you see her, and that's the person she'll want to be.

Be extremely careful. Many times fathers make innocent comments that are hurtful to daughters. If you comment on her weight, physical appearance, athletic prowess, or academic achievement, she'll focus on her "external self" and worry about retaining your love through her achievements and appearance. Your daughter wants you to admire her deep, intrinsic qualities. Keep your comments positive, keep them on these qualities, and you can't lose.

Instead of saying, "I love you because you're so beautiful," tell her that you love her because there is no one else in the world like her.

Expressing emotions can be tough for men. But loving people is tough. If you aren't comfortable verbalizing your love, you can write her a letter. Girls of all ages love letters and notes. You might think they're corny, but I guarantee that she won't. Ponder your love for her, write it down in a very simple way, and leave the letter on her bed, in her backpack, in her drawer. It doesn't matter. She'll take praise from you anywhere, anytime. If you doubt my advice, do an experiment.

Write a note affirming her in any number of ways. Leave it where she'll find it. Then six months or a year later, go look for it. I'll guarantee you'll find it tucked away in a special place. She'll save it because she wants to be connected with you and loved by you, always. Even if your feelings toward one another change as she grows older, the words on the paper won't change. She needs these words.

Fences

In general, men are better at building fences than women are. I don't mean literal fences, but the walls and boundaries your daughter needs around her world.

When she is two years old, you define your daughter's territory: what is safe to do and what isn't. You establish how she can behave and how she can't. You create borders around her movements, language, and behavior because you don't want her to get hurt.

As she grows older you take some fences down or move them back. You give her latitude to roam, but she is always under guard. When she is thirteen, some fences need to be reinforced—especially because she might try to break them. You can't let her do that, because she's still a kid. And because the boundaries make her feel loved.

Daughters with a curfew know that someone wants them home and is probably waiting for them. Daughters without curfews wonder. Girls who are told to mind their language know their parents want them to grow up to be well-spoken women. Girls who grow up swearing in front of dad don't believe that.

Teenagers often try to manipulate fathers by accusing them of not trusting them. And this kind of manipulation often works. Tell your teenagers that the boundaries you've erected aren't about trust, but are about keeping them safe and moving them in the right direction. We all have boundaries that we respect because life is safer that way.

I recently spoke with Steve, a police officer in California. He can tell story after story of teens getting in trouble because their parents either were absent or weren't tough enough to put up the boundaries they should have.

We talked about how difficult it is for parents to be realistic about their own children. Because we *want* them to make good decisions, we *assume* they will. We want to believe our kids are stronger, more mature, and better capable of handling situations than other kids. And that's when mistakes happen.

Steve told me that he remembered when his sixteen-year-old daughter, Chelsea, wanted to go to the movies with her seventeen-year-old boyfriend.

"I knew him," he continued. "He was a great kid. They both were."

He told Chelsea that she could go, but only after they had a chat.

"She rolled her eyes and groaned." He laughed. "I know she thought I was going to lecture or preach to her. So I simply said I had a few questions to ask her.

"We sat down and I asked her what she would do if her boyfriend suddenly changed his mind and decided to go to the drive-in instead of the theater. 'I'd go to the drive-in,' she said.

"'Okay,' I said. 'Let's say you go and he jumps out of the car, opens the trunk, and pulls out two six-packs of Budweiser. What would you do then?'

"Chelsea told me she wouldn't drink. She got a little agitated. She told me I knew her better than that, and that she'd proven that she could be trusted. She started to get up from the table, but I said, 'Hang on, Chelsea, we're almost done. Only a couple more questions. Would you let him drive you home?'

"'Well,' she said, 'I would if he wasn't drunk, and if he was, I'd call home and ask you for a ride.' She smiled and thought that was it, but I said, 'Good. I hope you'll always call home when you need to. But how many beers do you think would make Tom unable to drive?'

"'Come on, Dad,' she said. 'It's not hard to tell: maybe six or seven beers.'"

Chelsea's answer, he admitted, caught him off guard. She had given the right answers all along. Then, bingo, he was reminded she was sixteen, and that meant he needed to move in the fences.

Loving Chelsea meant no drive-in, no beer, but one movie at the theater, and then straight home afterward.

Fathers often overestimate their daughters' maturity. We're all taught that girls mature faster than boys, which is partly true. But researchers now know that some girls don't develop adult cognitive skills until their early twenties. This is explained in an article published by the Medical Institute for Sexual Health:

> Dr. Jay Giedd, chief of brain imaging in the child psychiatry branch at the National Institute of Mental Health, has spent more than thirteen years performing MRIs and studying the brains of more than 1,800 kids. Through high-powered MRI technology, he has discovered that the adolescent brain, while fully grown in size, is still a long way from maturity.
>
> Long after the size of the brain is established, it continues to undergo major stages of development. One of the last regions of the brain to mature is the pre-frontal cortex— home of the so-called "executive" functions—planning, setting priorities, organizing thoughts, suppressing impulses, and weighing the consequences of one's actions. This means the part of the brain young people need the most to develop good judgment and decision-making develops last!
>
> According to new studies, the pre-frontal cortex usually does not reach a level of genuine maturity until someone reaches their mid-twenties. "It's sort of unfair to expect [teens] to have adult levels of organizational skills or decision-making before their brains are finished being built," says Giedd.[1]

This is another reason fathers need to be protective of their daughters.

Many fathers fear that enforcing rules on their daughters will only make them rebel. Some daughters do rebel—but not because of rules. They rebel because the rules aren't balanced by anything else. Rules can't be the center of your relationship. That's where love comes in.

But you do need the rules. I have seen girls whose parents set no limitations end up in juvenile detention centers. And I know most conscientious fathers (and mothers) err on the side of being too lax.

The risks to your daughter can be close to home. For example, no seventeen-year-old girl—no matter how well behaved—should be at home alone overnight. Why? Because other kids will find out she's alone and come over to the house. Chances are, she won't call any adult (let alone the police) for help—and no seventeen-year-old has the cognitive skills to make consistently good judgments. This has nothing to do with character or intellect. It's simply too easy for a girl to assume that having a few friends over is no big deal. Sure, maybe nothing will happen. But what if it does? She shouldn't be put in that situation.

Silence

Most daughters tell me their fathers listen better and preach less than their mothers do. But there's a catch. It's harder to get a father's attention. Mothers are better at reading a child's mood and are more likely to ask questions.

But it is your attention she wants, because she senses the strength and concern behind your silence. She senses that you are genuinely interested in what she has to say—and that makes a daughter feel significant, mature, self-confident, and loved.

Many fathers complain that their teenage daughters won't talk to them. They're usually wrong. It's just that these fathers have discouraged their daughters from talking to them. Daughters won't talk if they know the result will be only constant reprimand and correction. Daughters want their fathers to listen while they unravel their own tangled feelings and beliefs. If a daughter can trust her dad to listen, she will come to him again and again to talk.

Listening is tough, particularly when the words don't make sense and the ideas seem superfluous. But listen anyway. Sit down. Look her in the eye. Don't let your mind wander. And you'll be rewarded with a daughter's trust, love, and affection.

Time

Being a father means giving up your time without resentment. It's hard, I know. Men spend most of their time working for someone else. When you come home and there are even more demands on your time, you might feel like distancing yourself from your own family.

Your daughter realizes this, and because she wants to please you, she might not tell you how much she needs your time. So *you* have to take the initiative to spend time alone with her.

I realize that many good fathers feel pressured regarding time. There isn't enough, for any of us, and the lack of time or misuse of it causes great anxiety. We carve out time slots for our kids, and we don't want to waste that time. We want to ensure that it's productive and meaningful. And that only adds to the pressure.

But spending time with your daughter shouldn't be full of pressure, because she doesn't need you to *do* anything; she only needs to be with you. So don't worry about finding activities to entertain her. She doesn't want to hitch a ride on your golf cart. (And she certainly doesn't want to share you with the television.) All she wants is your attention. And she needs it on a regular basis.

Many fathers are uncomfortable being alone with their daughters. One-on-one time can be tough. But if you start dad-and-daughter time when she's young, it will bring you closer when she's an adolescent. The rewards can be enormous. Daughters often say the most meaningful conversations of their lives were one-on-one with their dads.

Keep one-on-one time simple. Avoid activities that put you in competition with your daughter. Always use this time for emotional balance, for relaxing and having fun. You can work out conflicts later.

If you think this is a waste of time, think again. One of the primary treatments for girls with eating disorders is to spend time like this with their dads. These fathers learn not to harp on problems, but to focus on having fun together, which helps daughters center themselves on this healthy relationship and disassociate their illness from who they are. Eating disorders can make girls agitated, manipulative, and volatile; they can make them lie, yell, break down in tears, and be disrespectful. In short, they can be really hard to deal with. So telling a dad to spend time alone with his daughter might not be what he wants to hear. But spending enjoyable time together teaches father and daughter that beneath her illness, and the misbehavior it can cause, she is still a girl to be loved, and that's the first big step toward her recovery.

As we will see in a later chapter, "family time" has diminished over the decades. One result of this is that communication between family members is worse than it used to be. Over the last forty-five years, the amount of time kids spend with their parents has gone down by ten to twenty hours per week. At the high end, that's almost three hours *a day* gone from your relationship with your children.

For divorced parents, the challenges are even greater. And for fathers (who usually don't have custody of the children) the time lost can be enormous. But you need to find those small pockets of time to be with your daughter. That time can make an enormous difference to her. Your physical presence alone can make her feel protected.

Some of the best medical literature about keeping kids out of trouble comes from the Add Health Study. With overwhelming evidence, the study shows that kids who feel connected to their parents (and who spend more time with them) fare much better than kids who don't. Parents keep kids out of trouble; parental influence can be more important than peer pressure; and specifically, daughters who spend more time with their fathers are less likely to drink, take drugs, have sex as teenagers, or have out-of-wedlock babies. Your time with her matters.

Will

"If human love does not carry a man beyond himself, it is not love. If love is always discreet, always wise, always sensible and calculating, never carried beyond itself, it is not love at all. It may be affection, it may be warmth of feeling, but it has not the true nature of love in it."

So spoke the great teacher Oswald Chambers at the turn of the twentieth century. Love, he taught, is a passionate feeling that needs to suffuse our relationships with others. It can't be calculated, it can't be turned on and off, and it has to be ever-present in your relationship with your daughter. But as a dad, you know love also requires work and recruitment of the will. Romantic feelings wax and wane between lovers. Even the most perfect love requires an act of the will. If it is to survive, it has to be nurtured, cared for, developed, and practiced. And it has to live in the real world. Real love is gritty. It sweats and waits, it causes you to hold your tongue when you want to scream obscenities in anger, and it causes many men to accomplish extraordinary feats.

As natural as the love you feel toward your daughter might be, there will be challenges to that love, from crying squalls when she's a baby, to kindergarten tantrums, to other stresses of growing up that might show themselves in disrupted sleep patterns, moodiness, or ugly language. Your daughter, whatever her age, responds differently to stress than you do. If you're upset, you might watch a football game, go for a jog, or go fishing. Not her. She wants to spill her tensions on you. It makes her feel better. So be ready—and don't be surprised if she does this from an early age. Many parents ask if daughters can experience PMS before puberty. My answer is yes. It doesn't make good medical sense, but I see it repeatedly.

It's inevitable, too, that your daughter will go through stages. She'll draw close to you, then she'll pull away; she'll adore you, then she'll want nothing to do with you. You need to love her not only when she is your sweet, affectionate girl, but also when she's a real pain in the neck to be around. When she's moody, you still need to communicate with her—and you need to keep yourself from exploding when she's disagreeable.

How do you do that? Discipline. Grit. Will. If you need to distance yourself emotionally for a time, do it. If you need physical separation for a bit, okay. But always come back. Will, patience, calm, and persistence will pay off in your relationship with her. Nothing better expresses serious love than this combination of qualities. Let her know that nothing she can do, even running away, getting pregnant, tattooing her ankle, or piercing her tongue, can make you stop loving her. Say that if you need to.

Love, as Mr. Chambers said, must push us beyond ourselves. It will jab every sensitive part of you and turn you inside out. Having kids is terrifying because parenting is like walking around with your heart outside your chest. It goes to school and gets made fun of. It jumps into cars that go too fast. It breaks and bleeds.

But love is voluntary. Your daughter cannot make you love her or think she is wonderful. She would do that if she could, but she can't. How you love her, and when you show it, is within your control.

Most parents pull away from their teenage daughters, assuming they need more space and freedom. Actually, your teenage daughter needs you more than ever. So stick with her. If you don't, she'll wonder why you left her.

I know this is tough stuff. But it's worth it. Here's the story of one father who recruited his will to love his daughter at a tough time and won.

❖ ❖ ❖

When Allison started seventh grade, she changed schools. Her family had recently moved and Allison hated the move. When she got to her new school, she found a few classmates who shared her sour outlook on life. One kid's father drank too much, another's mother moved away. She and her friends got into a lot of trouble drinking and smoking dope. After several months of counseling and hard work, Allison's parents decided that she needed to leave school—and even home—and receive treatment at a residential home for girls. She was furious. She began lying to her parents and stealing. This was particularly tough for her father, who was a new, yet highly respected, businessman in the community.

He told me he felt terribly guilty for moving his family and wondered out loud how he had failed Allison.

The weekend before she was to be admitted to the program, John did something brilliant. Painful, but brilliant. He told Allison that the two of them were going camping on an island with very few other people. I'm sure that this wasn't exactly fun to think about for either of them, but he took charge. Miraculously, Allison packed her own things (John was expecting that he would have to). She even put her gear in the car, and off they went.

Neither spoke during almost four hours in the car. They ferried to the island and set up camp. Over the weekend they talked only occasionally. They went for hikes, made pancakes, and read books. (I'll bet John chose an island because he knew she couldn't run away.) No earth-shattering conversations occurred between them. As a matter of fact, John said he didn't even approach the subject of her bad behavior or the treatment program. They just camped.

After they returned home, Allison left for an eight-month stay at the nearby residential home. She improved, her depression lifted, and eventually she pulled her life back together. Nevertheless, her early high school years were tumultuous, and John's relationship with his daughter remained strained. But by the time she turned eighteen, their relationship had turned around. And by the time she graduated from college, he said, his friends were envious of his relationship with Allison.

When she was in her early twenties, Allison talked to her father about those difficult years. She felt guilty for causing her parents so much hurt. She told them she was sorry and that she couldn't believe they had put up with her.

I asked her what had made the difference in her life. Without hesitation, she told me it was the camping trip with her dad.

"I realized that weekend that he was unshakable. Sure, he was upset, but I saw that no matter what I did I could never push him out of my life. You can't believe how good that made me feel. Of course, I didn't want him to know that then. But that was it—the camping trip. I really think it saved my life. I was on a fast track to self-destruction."

❖ ❖ ❖

You will always be your daughter's first love. And what a great privilege—and opportunity to be a hero—that is.

Words, Fences, Silence, Time, and Will: What Difference Do They Really Make?

In Chapter One you read a litany of the troubles all American girls face. Now let's get very specific. Before your daughter graduates from high school (maybe even from junior high), she or many of her friends will have dieted. Most girls go through a period of obsessing about their weight, and many develop full-blown eating disorders. In my experience, mothers understand why and how their daughters get wrapped up in the ultra-thin craze. Dads often scratch their heads—even as dads are crucial to the recovery process—and wonder, "What's the big deal? Forget it, just put some food in your mouth, and get on with it." You, men, are so very lucky in this regard. Your daughter, tormented by internal demons (in that active interior life that all girls have), can't just "get on with it."

Eating disorders are at an epidemic level in our country. These include anorexia nervosa, bulimia nervosa, binge eating, and obesity. The common element in each is an obsession with food: either to restrict it, get rid of it, or indulge in it. The chances are excellent that your daughter will fall into one of these categories before she graduates from high school. So what can you do to prevent any of these from happening?

First, it will help you to have a basic understanding of the etiologies of these diseases. There is no need for you to be a psychologist or an expert, but it will help if you can watch life from the eyes of your little girl: to see what she sees, hear what she hears, and understand what she feels. Is this really necessary? Yes, it is really necessary, because according to all the best scientific research, no one has a more powerful effect in preventing and helping her recover from eating disorders than you do.[2]

Anorexia nervosa and bulimia nervosa are complicated illnesses. They are incredibly painful for parents and they are frustrating for physicians. To help you grasp what's going on in a girl's mind, I am going to simplify a complex issue into a few workable concepts and tips to help you protect your daughter. According to the National Eating Disorders Association, the major factors that cause eating disorders are low self-esteem, feelings of inadequacy, depression, anxiety, difficulty expressing emotions, troubled family relationships, cultural pressures glorifying thinness, and physiological or genetic factors. Of course, other factors can contribute, and it's important to realize that no two eating disorders are the same; they are as varied as girls' personalities. Sadly, 90 percent of eating disorders (anorexia and bulimia) occur in girls and women ages twelve to twenty-five, when their developing minds and bodies are most vulnerable. It is imperative to understand that each of these diseases must be taken seriously—because they are life-threatening. *Anorexia* (which literally means loss of appetite) *nervosa* (which means neurosis) can lead to decreased heart rate, decreased blood pressure, brain damage, and heart failure.[3] *Bulimia nervosa* is characterized by binge eating followed by some method to avoid weight gain: vomiting, laxative abuse, or enemas. Though harder to recognize from the outside, bulimia can be equally devastating. It can lead to rotten teeth, erosion of the lining of the esophagus, stomach damage, chemical imbalances, heart failure, and death. So if you suspect your daughter has either of these disorders, or even if your instincts tell you that she is at risk, get help for her right away.

Eating disorders are usually part of a process that starts with changes in her thinking, then in her feelings, and finally in her behavior. So let's peer into her mind and see what she might see on a typical day, as she records it in her diary.

I go to school for my first hour class in Algebra. I'm nervous because I'm not sure if I got my answers right. The teacher calls on me to give my answers and my heart sinks. I'm frozen in my chair. Tim is sitting three chairs away and I know he thinks I'm stupid now. Or if not now, he will in a minute. Ugh, and my shirt's ugly. I don't want everybody to stare at it. Get up.

I get up and give my answers. Most were right. Two were wrong and everybody laughed. Why should they? I'm smarter than those jerks. I'm so glad it's over. Anna and Jessie sat with me at lunch. They're my best friends. I can talk to them about anything. Anna's on my soccer team. Jessie bugs me because she only eats salad for lunch. She doesn't put dressing on it, and I feel guilty that I do, because she's thinner and prettier than I am. Her clothes are size 0. She's so lucky. I don't like shopping with her because she makes me feel fat. I guess I am. I'm a 2, but I could be a 0 if I tried.

I hate sitting next to her, and I feel guilty about that too. All the guys come up to her and drool. It's sick. I mean, Anna's a whole lot more fun and pretty. Maybe it's because she's strong and athletic. Maybe they think she's ugly. They must. But they don't talk much to me. I hate being shy.

I couldn't stop thinking about the boys and Jessie. I should start eating more salads. I really would feel so much better if I lost a few pounds. I'll start running. That'll help.

Let's pick up the diary a month later.

This feels great! I've lost 10 pounds in only 3 weeks. It's not so bad. I run every day. I'm almost a size 0. My friends tell me I look great. I'm still having trouble with Algebra, but who cares? I read *Cosmo* today, picked up all sorts of good advice about what guys really like, and I felt really good. I love the clothes in *Cosmo*. I want to be an actress, if I could just get over my shyness and lose some more weight. I'd be really good, I know, and I'd get to wear cool clothes. I know this sounds stupid, but sometimes I like to pretend that I'm in *Cosmo* and that I'm being interviewed. But I'd never make it now. No way, they're much skinnier and toned than I am. Got to keep at it.

Two months later:

I'm confused and I feel guilty. I went to this website and they said that throwing up would make me lose weight faster. I tried it. It was kind of gross. But, it's working, so I'll keep going. My running too. I'm up to 5 miles a day. Sometimes I like to run, sometimes I hate it. My dad's getting on my case. What's wrong with me, he asks? He says I'm irritable. Maybe it's cuz I don't have periods anymore. I don't know. He looks at me funny. We don't get along as well and I kinda avoid him because I don't want him to find out about the throwing up. No way, no one can know.

Four months later:

School's going horribly. People drive me crazy. They get on my nerves. I don't want to go to school, but my dad makes me. He thinks I have cancer or something. I hate doing my work. I don't know what the problem is—I just can't concentrate. At least I've passed a size 0. Food tastes awful. I can't have it. Every day I leave the house before my parents can see that I haven't had breakfast. I don't want to go to school. Anna and Jessie are acting weird and they don't seem to want to do anything with me anymore. Maybe they're jealous but why? I mean, they're much thinner than I am. I mean, I've lost some weight, but if I can only get rid of the lumps at the top of my thighs, then I'll start eating again. I can't focus on math or science because they're in the morning and lunch comes after. I can't stop thinking about what I should eat for lunch. Should I use dressing? Jessie doesn't. Nope, I can't. I can do better than she does. I'll just have water.

Lunchtime came. Anna and Jessie came over. I wanted to run away. I hate watching people eat. They are so lucky. They can eat, but I can't. I mean, I guess I could but I want to be different. I drank water and since I had some free time, I snuck in a run. My teacher got mad and made me go to the principal's office because I was half an hour late to class. Who cares?

Six months later:

My dad and I got in a real bad fight. I don't know what's wrong with him. He doesn't get it. I mean, what's wrong with losing a few pounds? He won't hug me anymore cuz he says it bothers him. I know why, I'm too fat. I flunked my French exam the other day. I hate French. I can't wait till school's over. I just want to be able to sleep as much as I want. I'm so tired. I better take vitamins or something.

Something weird is happening. Whenever I take a shower, a lot of my hair's coming out. My stomach hurts all the time. I guess it's cuz I'm eating too much. Two days ago I had a salad and yesterday I had some green beans. I know I shouldn't have. They made me have a stomach ache. I get nervous when I run too. I used to be able to run 6 to 8 miles, but I've dropped back to 3 because I felt this funny bump in my throat, kinda like my heart was beating up there. I can't tell anyone I've dropped my mileage because they'll think I'm lazy. I know they think I should lose a few more pounds and I don't want them to think I'm not trying. This feels good, but it feels horrible too. I can't stop thinking about running more. I can't stop thinking about what I shouldn't eat. It's like there's a monster in there, running my mind. I need to just sit in my room and figure all of this out.

Seven months later:

I think everybody around me is crazy, I swear. I mean, I think everybody was overreacting—especially my dad. He's here with me every day in the hospital and whenever he sees this tube in my nose, I can tell he's trying not to cry. This is so stupid, why don't they just get me out of here? When they leave, I'll turn the pump off. They're killing me. Don't they get it? I have to lose just a little more. My butt's too big. I would feel so much better if they would just let me eat what I want. I keep telling them: let me alone for 2 days and I'll eat. What is wrong with these people?

I don't know what happened but all of a sudden black came into my eyes, my ears were ringing, and my head hurt real bad. My dad says I passed out and fell off the bed. He says that some doctors ran in and hooked me up to machines. They even put something in my mouth so I could breathe. There were buzzers and whispers, tubes and wires. Someone was shouting at someone else about an injection of something. I can't really remember much. All I know is that they're crazy, they're all crazy. Don't they get it?

◈ ◈ ◈

That's usually how it happens. First, your daughter will hear things. She will begin to believe that her life really would be better if she were just a bit thinner. She will ponder and think of ways to accomplish this. The thoughts won't go away, because her friends want to be one size smaller (regardless of how they look), and so will she. She believes that if she were thinner, more people would give her attention, and she'd feel better about herself. Also, since many girls fantasize about being a model, posing for magazines, and acting on television or in the movies, they put a premium on being ever thinner and more beautiful. They diet and exercise, hoping they can live out those fantasies, or at least be more like the models and actresses they admire. Everywhere your daughter turns, at school, at soccer, at home watching TV, these thoughts will be reinforced.

Now, there is nothing wrong with eating right and exercising, as long as they're done for the right reasons and in moderation. But at-risk girls go to extremes. More than that, their characters change. An at-risk girl becomes intensely jealous of other girls who are popular and get all the attention. She thinks she's not popular because she's fat, or because there's something else wrong with her. She doubts herself, is full of anxiety, and is unsure if she can ever become popular. In an effort to feel better, prettier, sexier, to become more popular and get more attention, she diets and she exercises. Then her diet becomes more restrictive, then she starts starving herself, and then she starts forcing herself to vomit.

Researchers believe that eating disorders are hard to detect because most of them are subclinical.[4] Girls hide their eating disorders so well. Even while they are in a mental and emotional cage, stuck with obsessive thoughts and behaviors, they try to hide. It's especially hard for dads to understand that their daughters' addiction to starving feels so good to them. It's not like being addicted to alcohol or drugs, which have immediate physical warning signs that addiction will lead to misery—hangovers, "bad trips," crashes after drug-induced "highs." Starving, at least initially, brings great rewards. People comment on how much weight girls lose, how good they look.

Here's the good news: research also shows that you fathers, if you get involved and stay involved with your daughters, can play a pivotal role in *preventing* these horrible diseases, and your involvement is also crucial in curing them.[5] Let me say right up front that eating disorders are not a father's fault. They are complicated and many factors play a role in their appearance. But always remember that the strength of your relationship with your daughter can have a profound effect on preventing an eating disorder, curbing its progression, or healing your daughter if it catches hold.

Here are some practical things that you can do.

Make Time Count

The purpose of your time with her is to help her walk away feeling better about who she is. Research shows that daughters who feel a stronger emotional connection with their fathers feel more attached to them. And the more attached she feels to you, the lower the likelihood that she will be depressed or have an eating disorder.[6] One study concluded, "The asymptomatic group reported the lowest levels of depression and the highest levels of paternal attachment security."[7]

So how do you form that strong attachment? First, when you are with her, pay attention to her. Don't tune her out and think about something else while she's talking, don't ignore her when she's sitting next to you at a baseball game, and don't think she won't notice if you don't focus on her. Do activities that the two of you can enjoy together. Sure, there will be times when she'll drag you to the mall or you'll drag her to a car show. That's okay. But no matter where you are, make sure she knows that you know she's there. Ask her questions and listen to her. Girls hate feeling invisible. Without your attention, they feel unloved and insecure. Don't make the mistake of spending too little time or paying too little attention to your daughter. You could regret it the rest of your life.

Don't worry if your time doesn't go smoothly. Take her for a stroll in the park. If you end up arguing about her boyfriend, that's all right, because even arguing is a form of connection. You wouldn't argue with her if you didn't care about her—something she'll recognize, whether she confesses it later or not. Arguments aren't necessary for you and your daughter to figure each other out, but they don't necessarily hurt either. The one rule is that when the argument is over, it's over. Don't pick at it. End it, make up, and move on—all before the sun sets. And then take her out again.

When you take her out, you don't have to go far. Ask her to sit on the back deck with you, or help you in the kitchen, or work with you in the garage—even if it's just for a few minutes. The point is, when you show a genuine interest in being with her, she feels more attached to you. So give her time and attention, and you will come to see in short order that she really feels loved by you.

Listen to Her

Girls like to talk more than boys—including dads—do. It's healthy for girls to talk a lot, but it can be a problem for you, because men are experts at tuning people out. You have a lot on your mind, you're less verbal than women are, and all of us, particularly when we're really busy, have a tendency not to give people our full attention.

So when you're together, she'll probably do most of the talking. Just listen patiently—and don't try to fake it. Daughters can tell right away when dads aren't listening. Exactly what you don't want to happen—have her get frustrated, give up, and emotionally distance herself from you—is exactly what will happen if she thinks you're not listening. Your job is to secure her attachment to you, and you do that by spending time with her and listening.

I can guarantee you one thing: if you listen to your daughter attentively for ten minutes every day, by the end of the month you'll have a completely new relationship with her. Do what you would do naturally, as a man: spend more time listening than talking. If you listen, she'll feel loved. You'll be special to her because she knows better than anyone that most people don't listen. The emotional life of kids is egocentric, and that's where her friends are developmentally. So your daughter is dying to be heard. You don't need to agree with her, you don't need to have snappy retorts, and if you're called upon to untangle some very twisted thinking, don't worry. The very fact that you're there and spending time with her means that a lot of her confused logic will probably resolve itself on its own.

If you stay with her, look at her, and listen to her, she'll keep coming back for more. Her self-esteem will soar, her sense of loneliness will disappear, and she'll become more comfortable expressing her feelings. Finally, because you, the most important man in her life, obviously like being with her, she will feel more attractive. She'll think that boys who don't want to be with her have a problem (because you're smarter and more mature than they are). That's a good attitude for her to have, and one that can protect her in the long run.

Fence Her In

Boundaries and fences are a must for girls, particularly during the teen years. Remember that whatever she says, the very fact that you thoughtfully and consistently enforce rules of behavior makes her feel loved and valued. She knows that these rules are proof that you care. Equally important, they train her to build boundaries for herself and teach her that such boundaries are necessary. From your rules (and your own behavior) she will learn what is acceptable and what is not, what is good and what is bad, and what she will and won't do.

Many girls with eating disorders are kind, smart, and want to please others. Let your daughter know that the person she has to please is you. Let her know that your standards are hers, and that she is right to uphold them regardless of what her friends do. Guide her and help her reject harmful behaviors. Make it a habit and she will too. Girls who have been encouraged to be strong athletically, emotionally, intellectually, and physically learn to take over the role of encouraging themselves to succeed. They don't suddenly go crazy or become weak-willed. The same is true with your daughter's character. The discipline and standards, the fences and boundaries that you have integrated into her life will become her own.

The Importance of Words

We've talked about the importance of listening; equally important is what you say. What you say can actually help stave off eating disorders. Here's the key: Listen hard and long. Then listen some more. Try to understand what she's up against, what's going on inside her, and what struggles she feels. Remember that when you're a kid, very small things can seem like very big ones. Dads are important to help daughters put things in perspective.

As a father, you might see yourself primarily as a provider, but you also have a powerful role as a teacher. In fact, it's your biggest role. So go ahead: don't hoard your wisdom, share it with her. Give it to her in pieces, when you think she's ready for it, when it's relevant to whatever she's struggling with.

Be calm, patient, and frank. Tell her that women in magazines aren't the best role models, that people who judge everyone on their looks probably have terrible self-esteem issues. Tell her that what matters is not how thin someone is, but what her character is. And tell her what is great about her, what you like about her, what you hope for her.

Here are some extremely important don'ts. They apply to you and they apply to any close friend or relative interacting with your daughter, so feel comfortable telling other adults what they can and cannot say to her. That's your right.

1. Don't comment frequently on how she looks.
2. Don't comment on your own need to diet.
3. Don't make derogatory comments about her body. Many fathers think they are being cute when they tell their daughters

they have cute butts, strong thighs, and so on. Some get quite crude and name their daughters' body parts. Don't. It will come back to haunt both of you.

4. Don't comment frequently about her clothes. Yes, you should have standards for what she can and can't wear, and about makeup. But you don't ever want to communicate to her that appearance is a high priority. (This is one reason why school uniforms are a good idea. They set a basic standard for neatness and appearance, while establishing right away that everyone is equal and that focusing on dress sizes and styles is irrelevant.) Your daughter is just a kid and she really wants you to be happy with her. Let her know that you are, and that what matters is her, not what she wears.

5. Don't constantly focus on the importance of exercise. Yes, healthy exercise is important, but many Americans are egocentric about their exercise. They do it because they want to look good. Be very careful.

6. Don't make her feel she needs to do things to get your attention. Give it to her naturally, just as part of everyday life. Your daughter craves your attention and will do anything she can to get it. If you talk constantly about something, she'll head in that direction. So be careful what themes you reiterate to her; think about where they might lead. She's watching you, and she wants you to watch her.

The Importance of Will

Loving is hard. It might start off easy, but difficult kids, sick kids, daughters with attention deficit disorders or eating disorders can make love seem downright painful, requiring all the determination and willpower you can muster. Inevitably, there will be times when your daughter will drive you crazy, when you can't understand why she doesn't just stop emoting, or, if she has an eating disorder, why she doesn't stop starving herself, stop vomiting, stop exercising obsessively, stop being sullen and snippy. But willpower tells you to bottle up your rage and frustration in bad times, just as it tells you to bottle up your private tears when you see your daughter in her first formal gown, at her first piano recital, or when another girl calls her "fatty" on the playground.

To love your daughter well, to draw her close to you, to strengthen the bond between the two of you, you must have a will of steel. There will be times when you'll want to walk out. Don't. Take a break instead. There will be times when you'll want to scream. Don't. Have a plan for when you think you're going to lose it—and practice it. There will be times when you don't feel like expressing your love for your daughter. But do it. It will make you both feel better.

Think about the kind of dad you want to be. Sure, it will take hard work. But love isn't just about feeling good. It's about doing what you don't want to do, over and over again, if it needs to be done, for the sake of someone else. Love is really about self-sacrifice.

At the beginning of her life, she will feel your love. At the end of her life, you will be on her mind. And what happens in between is up to you. Love her extraordinarily. This is the heart of great fathering.

❖

Chapter Four

Teach Her Humility

Many parents roll their eyes at the word *humility*. We associate it with weakness, and we don't want our daughters to be weak or easily manipulated. We want them strong, self-sufficient, and independent. We want them to have self-esteem. These days, humility is a politically incorrect virtue.

But genuine humility is the starting point for every other virtue. Humility means having a proper perspective on ourselves, of seeing ourselves as we really are. It also means knowing that every person has equal worth.

Teaching your daughter humility is vital but tricky. You can't simply tell her that she's the same as her brother, the homeless woman on the street, and everyone else. Your daughter needs to feel unique and important in your eyes.

Teaching humility will demand more of you as a father than that. Humility doesn't make sense unless it is modeled. If you want your daughter to love reading, you must read. If you want her to be athletic, go for a run. The same is true with humility. If you live it, she will get it. Remember, she is a dry sponge following you around, waiting to see what you think, feel, and do.

Humility can be hard for many men to embrace. But not to embrace it is a dangerous game of self-deception. You and I know men who lack humility. Their lives become futile chases for things that don't matter, and neglectful of things that do.

I have known many successful men who embody extraordinary humility. They are successful professionally, intellectually, and emotionally because they understand that life is bigger than they are. Their work and their being fit into a much larger picture. Their successes not only benefit themselves—they also help those around them. A father's humility is a gift to his daughter.

The late English writer Alice Thomas Ellis was once asked, "What is the most important moment in women's history?" She answered, "The Annunciation." Why does your daughter need humility? What does it have to do with her happiness, self-esteem, and success in life? Here are some of the answers.

Humility Makes Her Feel Significant

I know it sounds like an oxymoron to say that humility will make your daughter feel more significant, but here's why it's true. To fulfill her potential, your daughter needs to understand who she is, where she comes from, and where she's going. And her understanding needs to be accurate.

Perhaps she has a talent for music. Perhaps she is smart or athletic. Like any enthusiastic parent, you are proud of her accomplishments. You pour money and time into her talents to strengthen them. You cheer for her at spelling bees, piano recitals, or basketball games.

Your support and encouragement are important. But you need to be careful too. If all you do is bolster her self-esteem with applause, she'll eventually see through that, and she'll wind up feeling frustrated. If she doesn't understand the virtue of humility, she'll start looking in the wrong places to try to feel better about herself.

Humility is seeing ourselves honestly. It keeps us in the real world. Because we want our daughters to excel at everything they do, to be prettier, smarter, better than everyone else, we can confuse our priorities—and theirs.

Our daughters don't need excessive praise to feel good about themselves. Deep inside, your daughter knows she's good at some things and not very good at other things. She often views her talents more realistically than her parents do, and the harder her parents push the praise button, the more she questions herself: Is this the reason my parents love me so much? Am I worth more to my dad if I play the violin better?

Another problem is self-centeredness. When family activities revolve around what we believe our kids "need" or "want" in order to feel better about themselves, we drive them to become self-centered. Many times girls gain a sense of superiority over their peers when they excel at something. And when this happens, they can become isolated from friends, peers, and family. Competitiveness creeps in. Their sense of superiority makes their world small and self-contained. They find no joy in what's around them. They focus on success, not on friends.

The writer Henry Fairlie was right to remark, "Pride excites us to take too much pleasure in ourselves, does not encourage us to take pleasure in our humanity, and what is commonly shared by all of us as social beings."

Pride is the opposite of humility. Remember what Dante wrote about the proud in the *Divine Comedy*? They burned in their self-absorbed pleasures, lonely and isolated for eternity. As Dante leaves them, the Angel of Humility comes to him, bringing splendor, peace, and contentment: "She bore about her so true an *umilita* that she seemed to say, I am in peace." Humility brings with it deep joy and satisfaction because it keeps us from becoming manically self-absorbed.

Don't let this happen to your daughter. Keep her world larger than herself and her talents. Gently guide her to recognize her strengths and limitations. Let her fail. Let her know that you still love her when she fails. Let her know that she's valuable not only for what she does, but for who she is. Here is your chance to teach her one of life's greatest lessons: people are valuable because they're human, not because of what they do.

But if you teach your daughter that improving her talent, intellect, or beauty will increase her self-esteem, you're setting her up for a terrible lesson, a lesson that can be exploited by others. When she goes shopping, what does she see? Millions of products promising to make her feel better. When she buys glossy magazines, she sees the sexy women on the cover as models to emulate. When she follows fad diets, she expects them to make her more beautiful, popular, and valuable.

Every week, your daughter is encouraged to buy hundreds of image-changing products—all of which focus on the superficial, not on what's real. Research has shown that, for example, people will buy outdoor clothing from signature companies like Patagonia not because they spend a lot of time outdoors, but because they want to *feel* or *look like* someone who spends a lot of time outdoors. Advertisers tell your daughter that her life will be more complete, exciting, and joyful if she buys their products, because they know the sales pitch works. It works because too many of our daughters have been set up to believe it. When fathers don't teach their daughters humility—that we are all created equal and are equally valuable—advertisers, magazines, and celebrities will teach them otherwise.

Vogue and *Cosmopolitan* will teach your eighteen-year-old (or ten-year-old) daughter that her worth is based on having an emaciated body with large breasts, wearing the newest and most expensive clothes, and being a "constant turn-on" to boys and men. Paris Hilton—a product of money, marketing, and diet—will be, to her, the quintessential beauty. Your daughter will read and absorb Paris's persona and try to imitate it. She'll use Paris Hilton to fill the emotional emptiness and social and spiritual vacuity she feels. That should be warning enough. But her longing to follow Paris and her ilk will draw your daughter toward a hatred of not having beauty, money, or a thin-enough frame. And she will be drawn away from a life of humility.

Can a woman be both gorgeous and humble? Can your daughter be brilliant, in passionate pursuit of a successful career, but still appreciate that she alone is not wholly responsible for her success? Absolutely. Humility will make your daughter's accomplishments shine all the more, and she will be more emotionally grounded, more satisfied, and happier than if she had tried to imitate Paris Hilton's life.

Marketers, Lindsay Lohan, and Paris Hilton draw your daughter into a life of emptiness. You can lead her in another direction by teaching her that she's valuable because of who she is—and because you love her. Her life is equal in value to yours and to everyone else's. Talent, intellect, and beauty are wonderful things to have, but they will never make her life more meaningful or give her more significance as a woman. Only humility will.

Humility Strengthens Her Relationships

It's hard to go through life without meeting someone who flaunts every gift you lack, or attending a dinner party where the conversation focuses on a subject you know nothing about, or being humiliated by a boss, a teacher, a parent, or even a friend. All of us have been made to feel stupid, contemptible, ill-suited, weak, and generally awful at some point in our lives by people who think they're better than we are.

Insecure people, we tell our daughters, call people names at school. And that's often true. Fat girls call other girls fat, dumb girls call other girls stupid, and plain girls call other girls ugly. Bullies try to set themselves above others and pounce on the presumed weaklings to show their superiority.

Humility, however, prevents bullying and being bullied. When your daughter recognizes that all humans have equal value and never esteems herself above another, she doesn't worry about asserting her superiority or take seriously a bully's taunts. She knows that our worth is not in what we do, what we have, or what we are capable of being, but in the fact that we are human. And bullies can't feel superior over people who refuse to feel inferior. Humility levels the playing field. This can make the insecure bully feel frightened. But it is the truth. And truth keeps us living in reality. It keeps us from being absorbed by a life of spite and self-destruction.

Girls who have the gift of humility are better placed to have deeper, longer-lasting friendships. With humility, your daughter is free to enjoy people for who they are; she'll have no haughty desire to cut people out of her life. This is extremely important because your daughter is a social creature. She needs other people. She needs adults to talk to, girlfriends to hang out with, and young men in her life to learn about relationships. No one can be happy in isolation. We were not made for isolation.

Humility is the foundation of all healthy relationships. Humility keeps each party in a relationship respectful, honest, and relaxed. If your daughter lives with humility, she will discover who she is and what significance her life holds. She will experience joy and contentment in her life. Your daughter was created to live in an intricate web of relationships. Humility keeps her inside that web. Self-centeredness and pride pluck her out of it.

Humility, for many Americans, is grounded in the teachings of the Judeo-Christian tradition, in which everyone is equal in the eyes of God because He created us and *wants* each and every one of us. Compared to God, who made us from dust, we might feel utterly insignificant. BUT (my favorite word in the Bible) God *made us*, so we have a place and a purpose, and He is willing to fill us with every good thing. All we have to do to escape the suffocating quarters of our own lives, to see ourselves with humility, is to recognize that we alone are not the source of all power, intellect, and talent. As we're told in the Beatitudes, "Blessed are the poor in spirit, for theirs is the kingdom of Heaven."

The great theologian Oswald Chambers says, "It is not a question of our equipment but of our poverty, not of what we bring with us but what God puts into us." God has filled your daughter with unimaginable gifts. Humility teaches her that these *are* in fact "gifts" for which she should be grateful, not proud.

Here's how one father experienced the joy of humility.

❖ ❖ ❖

At first Andy wanted to be a priest. He enrolled in seminary, but soon realized how much he wanted to be married. So he left seminary, went to medical school, and is now a highly esteemed physician teaching at a large university hospital in Pennsylvania.

Even though Andy abandoned the idea of becoming a priest, he never surrendered his faith. His love for God and his prayer life stayed vibrant. He had three daughters, and, as the years passed,

Andy knew that he and his middle daughter, Amy, had to take a trip together. He knew there was something they had to do.

When Amy was seventeen, he took her to the Dominican Republic as part of a team of fifteen volunteer health care workers. It was summer. The temperature rose to 101 degrees. They took a battered yellow school bus into a tiny rural village to offer the people free medical care.

The doctors filed into a cinder-block room, set up picnic tables as examination tables, and organized their supplies. The other volunteers sprayed for spiders, swept floors, and brought in lamps.

I was there and watched Andy work. He was remarkably patient and kind, always soft-spoken, no matter how much his hospital scrubs dripped with sweat.

One afternoon I saw him pleading with a woman. She responded angrily, on the verge of tears, and bolted from the room.

Andy collected himself, finished seeing his other patients, and then climbed into the old school bus before anyone else finished work. Amy went with him. Andy—a tall, strong man—sat down and covered his face with his hands. From a few seats back I overheard their conversation.

"I quit," he said to her. "It's time to go home, Amy. This was a terrible mistake."

He told Amy why the patient had run away. She had complained of chest pains. Though Andy is a lung specialist, he couldn't find anything wrong with her. He finally realized that the problem wasn't with the woman's heart or lungs—it was that her boyfriend regularly punched her in the chest. Andy told her she had to escape this abuse, to have her family take her to another village. Impossible, the woman said. She had no car, no bike, no money, and no family. (No one in the village had a car or a bike.)

Andy realized that there was nothing he could do. No medicine could cure her. And he could not protect her from her boyfriend's brutality.

Andy saw that poor, ragged woman as precious, maybe even more precious than himself, and that day on the bus in the sweltering heat, he cried. He had come face-to-face with his limitations in a way he never would have at his teaching hospital in Pennsylvania. There he had millions of dollars' worth of equipment to use whenever he wanted, he had wonderful supporting staff and infrastructure, and he could feel successful and powerful.

But that day in the village, all he had was himself and his limitations.

Andy talked about leaving the island a week early. "What's the point of being here?" he asked. "We can't really help these people. We don't have enough medicine or resources, and even if we did, as soon as we left, it would all go back to what it was. We have nothing to give. They need too much, and we aren't enough. No one is enough."

Amy said, "Yeah, Dad, but what about the love of God? We can bring them that."

"A lot of good that will do. They need water, food, electricity. They don't need someone to come in and tell them that an invisible God loves them. Where is He, then? They'll think He's cruel, abandoning them this way." Andy was now more angry than sad. The former seminarian questioned the character of God.

Neither of them spoke during the long ride home.

After dinner, I asked them about their earlier conversation. "What," I asked, "is the best we can give another?"

We finally decided that all we could give was hope—and that the only way to find hope was in God. Our purpose, then, was to show the light of God through our work. Our faith had led us here, and we needed to act on it.

The conversations that ensued between father and daughter brought them together on the big questions of life. In those conversations, Andy never said a word about living humbly and recognizing the value in everyone. That was assumed. His actions spoke for him. He simply lived his faith. And his daughter Amy followed.

Humility Keeps Her Balanced

Parents always say they don't care what their kids do as long as they're happy. As the mother of four, I understand this. I am incredibly selfish. If my kids are happy, I sleep better at night and enjoy my days more.

But think about this: Is that really what you and I want for our daughters? Should happiness be the goal toward which they work?

We all pursue happiness. It's our constitutional right. And happiness is a great state of being. But if you teach your daughter that happiness is her "arrival point," it could make her miserable. Here's why.

If she makes happiness her goal, you and she will discover that there are thousands of things that might make her feel good. Perhaps it's securing a Rhodes scholarship. Or maybe it's having a baby at fifteen. Or maybe it's the uninhibited expression of her beliefs to the point of wearing T-shirts that say "F— Authority."

The problem with making happiness her goal is the lack of guardrails. A goal of happiness can become a justification for self-indulgence. It can encourage selfishness. It can be how children become "spoiled." And, most important, it can actually lead to unhappiness, as there are no limits to a child's—or an adult's—

"wants," and these wants never ultimately satisfy a deeper need. So happiness remains out of reach.

The paradox is that happiness is truly found only when it is routinely denied. In my practice, the happiest girls are always the ones who live with humility. The unhappiest girls are the ones who are most self-indulgent in their pursuit of happiness.

If you think about this, it makes perfect sense. Self-indulgence is easy and takes no strength of character. Eating four pies feels good while you're doing it, but it will leave you feeling sick and make you fat. Watching soap operas rather than doing homework might seem like fun, but it won't prepare you for life after high school. Having sex whenever you want and with whomever you want might feel good, for a while . . . until you contract a sexually transmitted disease, or get pregnant, or find yourself deeply depressed. (I consider depression in teenage girls an STD, because it is almost always linked to underage sex.)

Humility teaches us rules and self-restraint, that we're part of a larger community and need to work together for the good of the whole. Humility teaches responsibility, and it teaches us to consider the needs of others. It tells us to look outward rather than focusing obsessively on ourselves, and it reminds us that we aren't the only ones who count.

The result is that girls with humility experience the real joy and happiness that comes only from strong, healthy relationships with family, friends, and others. We have rules to keep our relationships healthy. And among these rules is denying ourselves so that we can help others.

But everywhere your daughter turns, someone will tell her to indulge herself. She'll hear these voices from the radio, the television, the drug dealer, the bad boyfriend. All have their own answers to the good life. They call her away from what's real. They tell her no sacrifice is necessary—just take. No discipline is required—just enjoy. Indulge until you're full—or until you're empty.

All a father needs to do to see this firsthand is to take a walk around the mall. Look at the faces of the young girls. The expressions on many of their faces will be vacant, bored, lacking commitment, lacking purpose—and trying to find it in shopping or drugs or sex, anything to fill that sense of vacancy.

You don't want that for your daughter—not now, when she's six, and certainly not when she's sixteen. But that could be her future, unless you show her why she is significant, where her real value comes from, and why she needs others. That could be her future unless you teach her the humility that grounds her squarely in truth. Humility readies her for a life that has depth because it involves service and taking on challenges. It provides joy because it teaches her to look outward, not just inward. It gives her the wisdom to understand right from wrong. As her father, you need to give her the rules that keep her from harming herself and others. The rules you give her will direct her view of herself for the rest of her life.

Humility Keeps Her Living in Reality

Every child is born with a natural survival mechanism that causes him or her to be territorial. *Mine* is one of the cutest but most frustrating words any two-year-old chants repeatedly. As your daughter moves through her toddler years into her elementary school years and on into high school, she will probably go through some periods where she is more selfish, more territorial than others. Of course, some girls are less self-centered, less interested in fighting for personal ground than others. Some girls go into kindergarten terrible at sharing, wanting what other kids have and yanking things from their hands. This behavior will frustrate parents no end, particularly if they are generous people themselves. But when our girls are young, we all expect some selfish behavior because it's just a part of growing up.

Girls who insist on having their own way, who always want to be the boss on the playground, are tough kids to be around. They can drive other kids away. Selfishness is a bad habit, but training it out of girls (or anyone else) is a tall order. It takes time, discipline, and fighting against a popular culture that promotes selfishness as a virtue. Our daughters are bombarded by advertisements geared toward vanity and "me." Our daughters watch—and admire—pop stars who are as famous for their self-centeredness as anything else. Our daughters go to school and talk with friends about the newest and latest iPod, purse, or haircut. And they go to bed every night thinking they're lacking things that will make them happier. And the irony is, the more kids have, the more they want.

By far and away the most destructive lesson popular culture imbeds in our little girls' minds is that they *deserve* more. They have a right to things and your responsibility as a parent is to provide those things. That's what good parents, she thinks, are supposed to do in the twenty-first century.

I recently sat at a soccer game and listened to one father talk about his daughter, who was going off to college in the fall. She had been giving her folks a tough time for the last two years. At sixteen, she stated dating a twenty-year-old man who was "between jobs." Her father said, "That was mistake number one—letting that relationship continue."

As the year went on, she began running up her cell phone bill as high as $300. Her parents took her cell phone away. She was furious. Then she got into two car accidents and drove her insurance sky-high. Very appropriately, they made her pay for the increased insurance. This father was extremely frustrated because every time she got into trouble, and he and his wife responded to help her, it didn't seem to change his daughter's attitude. Now their daughter was angry because they refused to let her take her car to college and were making her pay part of her college tuition. "But I guess the thing that bothers me the most," said her dad, "is that she believes that it is our duty to give her this stuff and pay for college. She has even said that we owe her college. We are the parents and our duty is to get her through college, pay for the cell phone, and pay for her car because she honestly believes that those are her rights."

I could feel his frustration. His daughter wasn't just passing through an adolescent stage. She had a bad attitude that needed to change if it wasn't going to stick with her forever. She had good parents who now felt they were terrible parents. They questioned everything they did—everything they had done over her eighteen years—and wondered what in the world they did to produce such a selfish young adult. "She's a really good kid." Her father shook his head. "She is sweet, she is smart, and she is very affectionate. But sometimes I just hate being with her because she doesn't appreciate anything we've done for her."

Most eighteen-year-olds don't appreciate their parents' sacrifices and hard work. This is normal. What isn't normal is this girl's belief that she *deserves* what she has and that she has the *right* to continue to have it. Now many parents would look at her and think, "Wow, what a spoiled brat." I'm sure that's what her parents think. But in reality, she harbors a very corrosive and pervasive young adult belief that the majority of American kids probably have. The only difference is that she is vocal about it. Her problem: she has no humility.

She fails to consider the needs of others. It is as simple as that. Since she was born, her intuition told her to take what she needed, hold onto it, and get more. Those were the desires that drove her behavior. And everything in her environment fed that drive. Stores fed it by supplying fresh new things. Schools fed it by not holding her to high standards of behavior. And her parents fed it by desperately wanting to be good parents and giving her everything they thought she needed or desired.

Now, there is nothing wrong with giving our daughters every opportunity to discover their talents, to provide them with educational opportunities, and to give them the material things they truly need. We provide these things because we love our daughters. The problem occurs when year after year we focus on their needs and desires and how we can fulfill them, so that this becomes their focus as well. Our daughters become the center of our lives and their own. That intensive self-focus makes a daughter spoiled and miserable.

Humility is tough and it takes a lifetime to learn, so get going. Remember that if you don't, she will suffer more than anyone else. You need to set, as early in her life as you can, what the priorities for your family are. Do you want the center of the family's life to be the children? Should it be you, or you and your wife, or God? If you don't clearly establish your family's priorities, your daughter and your other children will. They can get very, very vocal.

From what I've seen in my office, the evidence is overwhelming: girls who are emotionally solid and intellectually and morally sound are girls with humility, who understand that they have to fit into the family, and that the family doesn't orbit around them.

What many parents don't realize is that giving in to a daughter's selfishness puts enormous pressure on her. When she's the focus, when she has the power to maneuver family schedules, vacations, or finances, when she has to decide what innumerable possibilities might make her happier, she becomes not only selfish but neurotic. Your daughter really doesn't want that much power. She's a kid. You're the dad. You should decide. You should set the priorities. When you bring realism into her life, you bring her comfort because you bring limits. When you teach her always to think about other people, to put herself in their shoes, to know that everyone—her friends, neighbors, and sister and brother—is important, you'll give her the gift of friendship and living to the fullest as a caring, social being.

If you teach your daughter to be good rather than simply happy, she will become both. Teaching your daughter humility is a wonderful gift. And it can be taught only by example.

Chapter Five

❖

Protect Her, Defend Her
(and use a shotgun if necessary)

Imagine you're on a hunting trip with a few buddies. The group heads to the woods and unloads the gear into the cabin. The cabin sits a mile and a half off a two-track road, and an early snow has just blanketed the trees and floor of the forest. You eat chili and have a couple of beers, build a fire, and sit and chat for a while. You decide to turn in so you can catch the deer early as they trek over the fresh snow.

As you tumble into bed, you notice a few magazines on the floor. You're relaxed, but not enough to fall asleep, so you grab a couple. The first is *Outdoor Life*. You've already seen that issue so you toss it back onto the floor. The next is *Playboy*, its pages wrinkled from frequent viewing. Your buddy's in the shower, so you flip through it. First you see titillating photos of gorgeous women with breasts the size of New York. You stop and stare for a moment, then flip the pages again. You're enjoying the photos, but they're not a terrific sleep aid. Finally you come upon the centerfold and your curiosity is piqued. You unfold it. Her body is amazing.

Then you see her face. *Wham*. It's your daughter's. You are so stunned that you can't close the magazine. You want to vomit, but you can't because you're shaking with anger, disgust, pain, and overwhelming grief. Your friend is drying himself off from his shower, and before he sees the magazine (which you realize he's already seen a thousand times), you sneak into the living room and stuff it into the black stove. Make it go away. You want to find every last magazine in the whole country and burn them all. But you can't.

This is a scenario I never want to happen to any father. But it's important because it helps you realize that you need clearly defined moral codes regarding sex. When it comes to your daughter, your standards must be clear.

It's also important because I cannot overemphasize the strong and seductive powers of the culture in which your daughter lives. The most aggressive campaign against your daughter's emotional and physical health is directed at her sexuality. She relies on your defense against that campaign. And fathers should know that the sexual messages your daughters see and hear today in popular culture are much more pervasive, powerful, and graphic than they were thirty years ago.

As uncomfortable as you may feel thinking about (and talking about) sexual activity regarding your daughter, you have to. She needs to know the moral code you have for her.

Many parents don't talk to their daughters because they feel guilty. I often hear, "How do I tell my daughter not to have sex in high school when I was sexually active in high school?"

Face it: whatever you did then does not disqualify you from being a good father now. Your daughter is at risk. You need to protect her. And honestly, she doesn't want to hear about your sex life.

This is tough stuff, but you have to do it. Every day she gets the wrong messages loud and clear. You need to speak louder and clearer. And your voice is the only voice she really wants to hear.

Here is the good news. Your conversations with her don't need to be detailed descriptions of sexually transmitted infections, or how to use birth control pills, or how many colors condoms come in.

What she wants to know from you is what the rules are. When is it appropriate to have sex and why? That's it. If that is all you ever impress upon her, it's good enough. You don't need to be an expert on anything, particularly when it comes to pills, condoms, or the peculiar sexual activities of teenagers. Just be her dad. Protect her budding sexuality and defend her right to modesty. Reiterate to her that sex isn't a simple bodily function—it is powerfully linked to her feelings, thoughts, and character. Tell her that a lot of what she hears and sees about sex is simply wrong. Keep it straightforward, loving, and respectable.

Institute a Defense Plan

Parents are the most important influence on their teenagers' decisions about sex.[1] The research telling us this doesn't specify "only parents who are good, kind, or excellent communicators." It says parents. Any parent.

But fathers in particular have tremendous impact on daughters. She compares all other boys and men to you. You're responsible for teaching her what to expect and what sort of behavior to demand from her male friends.

So how do you go about this enormous task? Think very seriously about her as a girl growing into a woman, a sexual being. When she is three years old, think about what you want for her when she is twenty. You must, because even when she's three you give her messages about her body—whether it's beautiful or chubby. And all these messages count.

Your daughter needs you to hug her often. If you are gentle, respectful, and loving, that's what she will expect from boys. And she needs to know—all the time—that you love her.

All girls from eleven years old on feel fat. They feel ugly, pudgy, pimply, and unattractive. Watch how your young teen stands. Most girls slouch if they're tall. If they're short, they wear platform shoes. Girls almost inevitably lack confidence in their appearance. So move in and hug her. The effect can be profound.

Few dads realize how important hugging is to their daughters, but I've heard countless girls tell me they had sex with a boy (not even a boyfriend) simply for the physical contact, because their fathers never hugged them or showed them affection. Her body starves for you to hug her. The need is especially raw during her teen years. Fathers often assume that their teenage daughters want to be left alone and don't want to be hugged. This isn't true—in fact, it couldn't be more wrong. She needs your touch during these years even more than when she was five. I know that popular culture tells you that teenagers "need their space," that teenagers are tricky and can leave you unsure what to do, that it might seem safer to opt out and simply do nothing, but that's all wrong. Your teenager needs you. It's far more dangerous to opt out of your daughter's life and do nothing than it is to be a close part of her life, and you know exactly what to do. Just be her dad: be confident, defend her and be supportive, and don't back away from hugging her.

Let her know that you see her. Let her know she's beautiful. Let her know that modesty is just another form of respect—for herself, for you, and for what she expects from boys—and that she shouldn't follow fashion trends and flaunt her sexuality just because other kids do.

It can be an uphill fight. Television commercials about ecstasy-inducing shampoo might not seem like a big deal to you, but you need to remember that your seven-year-old daughter is learning that being "sexy" is very important. The messages stream at her fast and furious. As her awareness grows, so does the power of these messages to destroy her innocent sexuality. By the time she's a teenager, you'll be tempted, like most parents, to just throw up your hands and turn your head.

But you can't. Your daughter deserves better than a life of promiscuity, or a life of modeling in pornographic magazines, which is exactly the sort of life the media are preparing your girl for. You have to intervene.

You might find it hard to believe that this devastating process is affecting the cute little girl who bounds out of her chair to hug you when you come home from work, or your third grader who is a rising concert pianist, or in your high school junior who has a chance for a scholarship to Yale. You cannot see it, but it is there.

The clothing industry acts as though innocence ends at age seven. Well before she reaches her teens, your daughter will be seeing PG-13 and R-rated movies—if not at your home, then at a friend's house. When she is nine or ten, she will hear about oral sex, and learn how HIV and other STDs spread. Her friends will show her teen magazines. She'll see *Cosmo* and Victoria's Secret catalogs, full of women posing seductively in sheer bras, thongs, and stockings with garters. When she is eleven or twelve, sex education pops up at school and she'll hear the words *condom, sexual abuse, heterosexual, homosexual, bisexual,* and *masturbation.* But most significant will be the time she spends with television, music, and the Internet. It will soar, and so will her exposure to sexual material.

"So what's the big deal?" you ask. Most parents desperately want to believe that these influences won't harm their children. As a pediatrician, I can tell you that they're wrong.

Teenage girls tell me routinely that they think they have to have sex to be accepted, cool, desirable, and sophisticated. They don't believe this because they're teenagers—they believe it because they've been told it, with nauseating repetition, from magazines, movies, music, and television from the time they were little.

I see this all the time in young girls. When they first try sex—not necessarily intercourse—they are curious and usually very disappointed. The disappointment makes them feel that something is wrong with them, because everyone else says it's great. So they try it again and again. In very short order they become emotionally dulled. Their instincts tell them that intimacy with another person has occurred, but their mind senses that no love was exchanged, no commitment was made, no emotional depth was involved. They become confused about love because sex came before love.

Sex separated from love creates a deep emptiness and a confusion about how to love. Repeated sexual acts—as mechanical acts—make love and sex no longer fit together. As a result, sexual satisfaction becomes impossible, and girls become jaded.

The good news is that when you teach your daughter that sex is intricately connected to every aspect of her being, she will believe you, because it intuitively makes sense to her. When you teach her that modesty is an important way to protect and honor her integrity, she'll understand that too, because kids have an innate sense of modesty. You have to be your daughter's protector and fight a culture that lies to her about sex and denies her right to modesty.

You can avoid daily fights over clothes, fashion magazines, music, or television by coming up with some ground rules. If the culture wants her to grow up too fast, slow it down. When it comes to clothes, let her pick them out within your guidelines. If you need some ground rules, adopt the sensible ones of my daughter's high school: high-necked blouses and below-the-knee skirts. Tell her that the point of your guidelines is not for her to be ashamed of her body, but to be respectful of it.

Should she read *Cosmo* or thumb through a Victoria's Secret catalog as an eight-year-old? No. Throw them out. If her mother gets them, she should keep them out of sight. Should your daughter go to sleepovers where "cool" parents let underage kids see movies rated PG-13 or R? No. Let other parents—and your daughter—know your standards. And have your daughter call home if they're violated. She'll be embarrassed, but she'll get over it. Defend your daughter's right to be a kid.

Defending her in a toxic culture is challenging when she is eight, nine, and ten. The challenges can intensify as she grows older. Notice that I said "can." This is because I've found that girls whose parents are reasonable, firm in their guidelines, and not overbearing understand early on that their parents are on their side and "get" what is going on in their world. That minimizes battles over movies, clothes, and the rest.

When battles do heat up, however, you have to kick into high gear. Don't be mean, loud, or aggressive. Kindness and strength in your beliefs work better. When your sixteen-year-old bounces into the kitchen with a bikini barely covering her large breasts and pubic area, smile and tell her that it's a gorgeous color, but the suit is too scant for her beautiful body. Tell her she needs to find a more modest suit that won't make other girls feel jealous. When she is twenty-five, she'll thank you.

Standing guard over your daughter's sexuality is tough. It is nothing short of war. But teaching her that modesty is a strength and not a commodity of the prudish will pay off with enormous dividends.

Protect Her from Sexual Activity

According to the Medical Institute for Sexual Health, in the 1960s doctors contended with basically two sexually transmitted infections—syphilis and gonorrhea. I was in elementary school. In the 1970s, when I was in college, chlamydia gained momentum. But really, no one paid much attention because the sexual revolution was taking hold and the last thing that college students wanted to hear about was chlamydia. In the early 1980s, when I was in medical school, HIV appeared, though it didn't make big headlines at first.[2] Then herpes simplex type 2 (genital herpes) increased wildly in the United States.[3] Again, you didn't hear about it in the news. As a medical student I remember being taught that cervical cancer was probably caused by an infection transmitted through sexual activity. Doctors had come to that hypothesis because they noticed that nuns never got it. In the 1990s we got the proof when researchers discovered that cervical cancer in women was caused almost exclusively by human papillomavirus, a sexually transmitted disease.[4] Pornography that encourages sexual behaviors previously frowned upon has helped spread disease. One study has shown that with the surge of popularity in oral sex among teens, herpes simplex type 1 (cold sores) now causes more genital infection than herpes simplex type 2.[5]

Over the last forty years doctors have gone from treating two STDs to treating more than twenty-five different types today. The true numbers depend on how you count. For instance, do you count HIV as one infection or two, since there are two strains of HIV?

And with HPV, there are eighty to a hundred strains. Fortunately, only twelve cause genital infections that can lead to cervical cancer. So does HPV count as one infection or twelve? The simple answer is that however you count, our kids are facing an epidemic of STDs.

Of the fifteen to eighteen million new cases of STDs that occur every year, two-thirds occur in kids under the age of twenty-five.[6] This is not okay with me, and as a father it should not be okay with you.

Don't assume that because your daughter is in a private school, or a parochial school, or a public school in a quiet small town that she is safe from all this. She isn't. The problem with bugs is that they don't discriminate. These infections cross all socioeconomic, racial, and religious barriers. Perhaps they didn't a decade ago, but this is a different day.

I am a pediatrician, and I have seen this epidemic develop even though I, like most of my colleagues, didn't immediately recognize it. Like many mothers and fathers of my generation, I grew up watching television, politics, and mass communication change with the Internet, and changes in marketing that started using sex to sell things to kids. Some of these changes bothered me, but my generation grew up discounting complaints from parents (including our own) about the awful influence of television and popular music, about radical and disrespectful kids, and about falling moral standards. So, when all of this happened, honestly, I didn't pay much attention. Change is part of life.

As a young intern and resident I worked with teens and their babies. I loved it. Having gone to Mt. Holyoke, an all-women's college, I was passionate about championing health issues for young girls. The best way to help them, we were taught, was to keep them in school and load them up with birth control: give them shots of Depo-Provera, get them on oral contraceptives, or refer to them to an ob/gyn who could insert Norplant under their skin. Preventing pregnancy is medically quite simple, but I got burned out working with kids who got pregnant anyway. So I decided to take a break.

In the meantime, my husband and I started raising our own three daughters. As they grew, they wanted to go to the mall and buy clothes. Their dad never took them, I did. And when they became young teens, they wanted to buy their jeans at Abercrombie & Fitch, because that's what their friends did. The moment we walked into the store, we were confronted by an enormous poster of a gorgeous and apparently naked twenty-something young man. Pretty soon I noticed that such sexualized marketing, directed at kids, was everywhere.

I shrugged it off until I noticed changes in my medical practice. Kids were starting sexual activity at ever-earlier ages. In the 1990s, I had patients who were sexually active in the sixth and seventh grades. Then I saw an influx of genital herpes. And I started seeing some horrible consequences.

One young mother delivered her baby not knowing that she had herpes because she had never had a herpetic sore. Shortly after birth, her otherwise healthy baby began having terrible seizures. She would turn blue, shake all over, and her breathing became so erratic that she looked like she was dying. An MRI of the baby's brain tissue showed that it was punctured throughout with holes. This baby was suffering the consequence of herpes—and here's the kicker: not only did the mom never know she had an infection, but her husband had contracted herpes many years before from a girlfriend and had tried to keep his wife "safe" throughout their marriage by not telling her.

The stories grew in number. I had a beautiful thirteen-year-old girl with advancing cervical cancer. Just before her fourteenth birthday, her gynecologist removed most of her cervix to halt the cancer's progression. If that poor girl gets pregnant now, she will have a high-risk pregnancy because her uterus might have difficulty keeping a baby inside.

I saw the pressure to have sex rise among kids—all kids. Parents sometimes find it hard to realize how things have changed, but they have, dramatically. In the 1970s most kids—teenagers—were not sexually active. Today, most kids are.

Even if we know this statistically, we can still fail to see how very significant it is. It's not harmless. The epidemic of STDs is life-threatening for your daughter. And the pressure on her to engage in high-risk behavior can be overwhelming. If your teenager is not sexually active, chances are that she will be treated as a social outcast, an unsophisticated, abnormal geek. You have to counterbalance that peer pressure. If you don't teach your daughter why she should defer becoming sexually active, she will start. And you'll need to teach her how to live up to your standards. That's just the way it is. Her friends are having sex, and even the nice guys she dates will expect it—very shortly after they start dating.

I noticed another trend in my practice. The early onset of sexual activity not only meant rising cases of STDs, but also meant that many of my young patients had had multiple sexual partners at young ages. And I saw something else: a rapidly increasing number of girls suffering from depression. I, like my colleagues, wasn't really trained to treat depression while I was in medical school. We left that to psychiatrists. We didn't have antidepressant medications or even the understanding of the roots of depression like we do now.

But I had kids as young as nine being dragged in by their parents because they knew something terrible was wrong with their daughters. Over time, I found an obvious correlation among my patients: if they were sexually active, they were at high risk for depression. So much so that I have come to consider depression another sexually transmitted disease. Studies couldn't confirm what I was seeing in my practice because studies weren't being done (though they would be later, as we'll see later). No one was paying attention to our kids.

Every day after I left my office, I was struck by a social and cultural disconnect. In my practice, I was seeing younger and younger girls ravaged by depression and sexually transmitted diseases. And at the mall and in magazines and on television, I saw a popular culture that didn't seem to care. Beautiful young girls were being seduced into sexual activity through brilliant marketing programs. Sex sold them clothes, shampoo, CDs, and pencils. Sex was sold to them in glamorous media messages. But outside that world of make-believe I saw sex giving young girls one infection after another. I saw girls falling into depression. I saw girls wanting to commit suicide.

And everyone was silent. We doctors were silent. Pastors never preached about sex. Priests didn't include talk about sex in their homilies. Parents didn't want to broach the subject. We didn't shield our kids. We took it for granted that they watched R-rated films splashing sex across the big screen. We left it to teachers to tell our kids to wear condoms, as if that were the answer to preventing depression or even the rising number of STDs (it doesn't work for all of them).

Finally, I began talking to my friends in medicine. "Are you telling girls about the risks of HPV? Or that chlamydia can cause infertility? Or what herpes can do to her baby?"

No, they weren't. Not because they're bad doctors, but for two reasons. First, they don't have time to go into lengthy discussions. Insurance companies pressure doctors to see many patients a day. Second, many doctors simply believe that talking to kids is no use. I hear all the time, "All kids are sexually active these days. Look around, there's nothing we can do about it."

So many simply give more shots of Depo, hand out packs of birth control pills, or plead with girls to insist that their boyfriends use condoms. I understand exactly why my colleagues do this. They feel overwhelmed. And so do I. But the truth is, many of us— physicians, teachers, and nurses—haven't been doing our jobs. We've been settling for damage control rather than trying to get kids back on the right course. Condoms are damage control. For me, that was no longer good enough.

I've studied the medical data. I've thought long and hard about my patients. I've talked to kids and parents. I've consulted with my medical colleagues. There is a solution to the problem of girls having sex too soon and with too many boys. The answer is: YOU.

Fathers can ensure that their daughters grow up with healthy ideas about sexuality. You can guide your daughter to make smart decisions about sex. You know that your teenage girl shouldn't be popping birth control pills, applying condoms, and being treated for STDs. She deserves better than that. If you as a father saw what I see every week in my medical practice, you would know what to do. And you'd succeed.

You need to know some data because your daughter needs your help. Take a look at what the medical research shows about your daughter and her friends.

⊕ If present levels of sexual activity among kids continue, by the year 2025 (fewer than twenty years from now),

39 percent of all men and 49 percent of all women will test positive for genital herpes.[7]

- Three to four million teens in the United States contract a new STD every year. That works out to approximately 10,000 kids *a day* who get a new STD.[8]
- Nationwide, gonorrhea rates are highest among girls ages fifteen to eighteen.[9]
- Of the top ten most frequently reported diseases in the United States in 1995, STDs accounted for 87 percent of all cases reported.[10]
- Nearly one in four sexually active teens is living with an STD at this moment.[11]
- Although teens make up only 10 percent of the population, they contract 25 percent of the STDs.[12]
- HPV causes 95 to 99 percent of all cervical cancer.[13]
- Some strains of HPV have been linked with cancers of the head and neck.[14]
- 45 percent of African American teens and young adults test positive for genital herpes.[15]

As a father, you might be shocked by these statistics. Good. We need to recognize that we have a very serious problem on our hands.

Angela's father did. If he had only known how miserable she became, he said later, he could have helped, perhaps before her depression got out of hand. When Angela was sixteen, she was dating a guy she thought might be "The One" (girls often think in these terms). Tack was older than Angela and was getting ready to graduate from high school and go on to college. Since they had dated for a month, Angela felt it was time to give Tack what he wanted. (One month, according to many teens, is a long time to date; it means the relationship is serious.) She was hesitant because she was a virgin. She had heard her friends talk about their sexual experiences and how disappointing they had been, and she really wanted to wait. But, she said, she didn't want to lose the guy she thought she might marry. (Fathers: this is exactly the kind of thinking—common in teenage girls—that you need to correct.)

They went to a movie, then to dinner. On the way home, Angela let Tack know about the decision she had made. He was thrilled. But before he got too excited, she told him that there were limits. She wanted to have sex but remain a virgin. And she wanted to be safe from infection, she said, so they had to stick to oral sex. That was fine with Tack—at least for the meantime, he said. So they did. In the back of his car, they exchanged oral sex.

Within a couple of days, he told his buddies. And, as guys and girls do, they talk to other people, and pretty soon most of their friends knew what Angela had done. They were amazed, Angela told me, because everyone in her class assumed she was the one who would never cave in to the pressure to have sex. She was too principled.

Four weeks later Angela broke out in sores around her genitalia. She had terrible pain urinating and even had difficulty sitting down. She had a horrific case of genital herpes—not caused by herpes type 2, but by herpes type 1 (oral herpes). Her intense pain lasted about four days and she needed narcotics to keep it under control. But even more painful to Angela was what Tack did. He not only told his friends that she had contracted herpes, he dubbed her "Miss Herpes," and she quickly became the girl that no boy wanted. She was humiliated and became very depressed. And remember, she endured this even while she still felt herself to be a virgin.

Six months later, in the bathroom in her home, Angela swallowed two full bottles of Tylenol. She couldn't take it anymore. Life just wasn't worth it. So she decided to give up and die.

Her parents were shocked. Angela had friends, excellent grades, and a promising future. They never linked her suicide attempt with Tack because they believed him to be a nice, respectable young guy. Surely he would never have taken advantage of her; they would never have had sex.

You can't bet your daughter's life on these kinds of assumptions. Too many parents who do pay a terrible price.

Here's another very important medical fact: the fewer sexual partners a girl has, the less likely she is to contract an STD.[16] And the longer she waits to start having sex, the more likely she is to have fewer partners.[17]

So, dad, you must help her, teach her to wait. Even Dr. Julie Gerberding, the head of the Centers for Disease Control and Prevention, says so. Recently she wrote a letter to Congress about preventing HPV infections in young women. Why? Because infections are out of control and women (particularly young women) bear the brunt of the problems incurred by these infections. I was privileged to testify at the congressional hearing, and this is essentially what Dr. Gerberding said: HPV causes cervical cancer in women, and we need to curb the spread of the virus. The best way, she said, was to have women reduce the number of sexual partners to as few as possible and to delay the onset of sexual activity as long as possible. Also, women should avoid sexual contact with an infected person. (The problem, however, is that HPV doesn't cause symptoms unless it is the strain that causes warts, and these strains don't cause cancer. Moreover, only 1 percent of HPV infections cause warts.)

Now, you may wonder, what about the gold standard backup plan? The panacea of all panaceas: the condom. Why didn't Dr. Gerberding simply reemphasize the importance of using condoms to prevent HPV infections? It's simple: condoms don't adequately protect against HPV because it is spread from skin to skin. For all that we in medicine, health clinics, and teachers in sex-ed programs have pleaded with teens to use condoms, and even handed them out for free, the sad fact is that condoms will not protect your daughter from all the risks she faces from sexual activity, including depression.

When parents and kids ask me, "Do condoms work?" I give them the best answer I have. I learned it from a colleague of mine who is referred to as "The Condom King." The man knows every piece of research ever done on condoms. The most truthful and medically accurate answer I can give is: it depends.

How well condoms work to prevent pregnancy and sexually transmitted infections depends on many factors. First, in order for them to be effective, condoms must be worn during every single episode of intercourse and they must be worn correctly every time they are used. Studies tell us that condoms are frequently used incorrectly.[18] Second, it depends on which infection you're talking about. The condom's track record is best with HIV and poorest with HPV.[19] Infections are transmitted quite differently. HIV resides in body fluids and it makes sense that a piece of rubber provides a pretty decent barrier against fluids. But a herpes sore, like a syphilis sore, can be on skin not covered by a condom.

Other factors are the problems of breakage and leakage with condoms, the way kids use them, and when they use them. Studies show that the longer a teen has sex, the less likely he is to use a condom.[20]

I believe that there are two reasons for this. First, teens don't think the way adults do. They really believe that bad things aren't going to happen to them. So they think that if they have sex a few times and they "didn't get" an infection, then they really aren't going to get one at all, ever. And often kids don't know that they're infected. Anywhere from 70 to 80 percent of the time, an infected person doesn't have symptoms. This percentage is true for herpes, chlamydia, and many other infections, the consequences of which turn up later. So the teen may really believe she's fine until she delivers a baby whose brain is shot through with herpes.

Second, I personally see that something inside kids—boys as well as girls—changes after they've had sex for a while, with one partner or with many partners. They don't seem to care about themselves in the same way. Many adopt a "why bother" attitude. I think they stop wearing condoms because they don't think they're at risk, and they don't really care if they are anyway. That's been my personal observation.

The bottom line for you, fathers, is that condoms alone aren't good enough for your daughters. Not by a long shot. So you need to move in and help your daughters in a way that your parents didn't have to help you when you were growing up. Life is different today—really different.

Depression as an STD

In my practice I spend a lot of time listening to and teaching teens. And I treat a lot of depression. It hits teen girls and teen boys, and the severity of depression covers a wide range. The link between teen sexual activity and depression is so strong that several years ago I started telling my patients that I couldn't treat their depression unless they stopped having sex, at least for a while. So many kids have been sexually active for so long that they think it's impossible to give it up for more than a few months. At first they balk and say they can't or won't. I tell them to try it for a week, and then come back and see me. They usually agree. At the next week's visit, I tell them that "sex messes with their heads." I have yet to hear any teen say that it doesn't. And I let them know that it is impossible to treat their depression adequately unless they stop having sex.

Researchers have known for a long time that teenage sexual activity and depression are linked, but the question was which came first—the sex or the depression. Depressed kids are more likely to engage in high-risk behaviors, and sex is a high-risk behavior. Last year, however, an excellent study was published on teens, sex, and mood. The researchers found that "engaging in sex and drug behaviors places adolescents, and especially girls, at risk for future depression." Also, they concluded that "because girls might have greater interpersonal sensitivity contributing to higher levels of interpersonal stress during adolescence, sexual activity likely contributes to experiencing stress."[21] The findings were so clear that the authors said that girls who are engaging in sexual activity should be screened for depression. The researchers' findings confirm my own clinical experience.

Really, it's common sense. Kids get depressed when they experience a loss for which they can't express a healthy emotion. This is very common with sexual activity. When a girl has sex, she loses her virginity, and very often loses her self-respect with it. Her boyfriend might tell the whole school, or make her do something she doesn't want to do or that leaves her feeling traumatized, or he might reject her in favor of another girl, or belittle her as no good at sex. You would be surprised at how many teenage girls have told me they have given up believing that sex can be enjoyable at all. Sex is sold to them as astonishingly wonderful. They are almost always disappointed at the reality, and rather than believe that everything the media has told them is wrong, they think something is wrong with them. So they try sex with different partners again and again. But the intimacy and romance they naturally expect with sex is never there. And all they do is become jaded and depressed. They lose self-confidence and self-esteem. And many feel they have lost a part of themselves that can never be retrieved.

These are girls who have grown up watching casual sex taken for granted on TV sitcoms. These are girls who read glossy magazines that are all about being sexy and having great sex. These are girls who watch music videos all about sex. When they actually experience it, and it fails to live up to their expectations, and they feel bad about it, they feel like they have failed as human beings. We adults have set them up for this.

Several months ago I was contacted by a pharmaceutical company that is working on the new HPV vaccine, which will be available soon and which doctors will recommend giving to girls before they hit puberty. Shortly after that call, I was contacted by a major news show that wanted me to comment on whether it was okay for girls to wear sexually suggestive clothing adorned with slogans like "I'm sexy" or "Want some?"

Can you imagine what would happen if cigarette companies marketed T-shirts to teens with slogans like "Wanna have a great time? Smoke!" or "Cigarettes rule!" How about if they did that while a pharmaceutical company prepared to launch a vaccine for young girls to prevent lung cancer, a vaccine that federal guidelines would ask us to give to every girl starting at age nine?

The fact is, popular culture is selling sex to our teens, resulting in skyrocketing rates of teenage sexually transmitted diseases and clinical depression. And don't expect anyone to do anything about it. The only person who can protect your daughter from the pimp culture of modern marketing is you.

And the best news is: you are a far more effective protector of your daughter than any condom, any sex-ed teacher, any school nurse, and any doctor. That's what kids tell us every day. They want to hear from their parents. They want their parents to tell them what's right, what's wrong, and what they should do. If you want your daughter to refrain from being sexually active as a teenager, you need to tell her why and how. You need to stay in the fight for her innocence and her mental and physical health. It's a fight you can—and that you must—win.

You can't rely on what they teach your daughter in school, as many parents do. For many years now—in the schools and in the media—we have been telling kids, begging kids, to use condoms, and all of this has coincided with rapidly rising rates of sexually transmitted diseases. The evidence is in: condoms are no solution.

The second option is to teach kids to postpone sexual activity until they are older. Some educators believe this is impossible, but the abstinence movement taken up by young people around the country is a hopeful sign. The popularity of these programs among teens shows that they are looking for help and encouragement to wait. I will never forget listening to a speaker at a medical conference a few years ago. She was onstage with a group of other teens discussing sex. One girl talked about being a teen mother. Another talked about why she had stopped having sex to become a "secondary virgin." But this young girl, probably seventeen or eighteen, told us, a room full of doctors, "We're confused. We hear all sorts of things from our friends and from teachers. It's hard, you know, figuring things out. But here's what really gets to me and a lot of my friends. We want some help but we don't always get it.

We have a real problem and you know what our problem is? YOU! You're the problem. You people, you doctors, and other adults, you don't think that we can do anything, do you? I'm sick and tired of hearing you talk about how out of control we are! So get this—we're not!" Then she turned and walked off the stage.

However shrilly she made the point, she was right. We have failed our kids. We haven't given them the rules. We've shrugged our shoulders at the epidemic of STDs among teens and said that there's nothing we can do but hand out condoms and immunize nine-year-old girls against HPV. But while we adults have given up, guess what is happening to teen sexual activity across the nation? It's beginning to decline. I see it in my own practice and in my kids' friends. They talk openly about sex (not the details, of course). You should know that many of your daughter's friends don't want to be sexually active, some probably aren't, and many others are looking for parental support *not* to be sexually active. They feel the peer pressure, they stay quiet to avoid it, and they're desperate for fathers to stand strong to help them.

Kids really do listen to us—and they have grasped at abstinence instruction because they instinctively know that it's right. If my own clinical experience is anything to go by, that explains why the incidence of teenage sexual activity has started to decline.

Summing Up

I don't want to belabor sex education in schools, but you need to know that your daughter is probably being taught a mixed message: that she should abstain from sex, but if she does have sex, she should make her boyfriend use a condom.

One seventh grade patient of mine told me that during sex-ed class her teacher encouraged them to abstain from sex until they were older, because it was dangerous and there were lots of diseases. But the teacher didn't explain how to avoid sex.

Then, quite to this girl's embarrassment, the teacher took a banana and showed the co-ed class how to use a condom. She passed the banana with the condoms around for all the students to practice.

"What do I do?" my patient asked me. "Should I wait or not? My boyfriend kinda wants to have sex. I guess everybody is, because my teacher told us all to be sure to use condoms. I'm confused."

I see this all the time: teens getting mixed messages from their schools, churches, and civic groups.

Be assured that your daughter hears a lot more about sex, birth control, abortion, STDs, and oral sex than you ever did at age thirteen. Some of what she hears will be right, some will be wrong, but I guarantee you two things. First, you might be opposed to what's being taught; and second, your daughter wants to know what *you* think about sex. Believe it or not, you have more influence than her teachers, Britney Spears, and Abercrombie & Fitch. You need to use that influence. If you think she should wait to have sex—even if she senses this from your behavior and beliefs rather than your saying it directly—she is more likely to wait. Studies show that kids who perceive that their parents don't want them to be sexually active or to use birth control are less likely than other kids to have sex as teenagers.

I'm a strong advocate of helping girls postpone sex for many reasons. I've given out birth control devices, including condoms, and it doesn't help kids get to a healthy place in their lives. Pregnancy might be avoided, but depression, infections, and low self-esteem all become bigger problems when we teach girls that birth control is the solution.

You need to decide what you want for your daughter and implement a plan to protect her. If you don't, the testosterone-charged boys at her school will implement quite a different plan.

What to Do

Here's a model plan, based on what I've seen—in research and experience—work for fathers.

1. *Teach self-respect early.* When she is three, begin telling her that her body is special. It is beautiful and she needs to keep it special. As she grows older, let her know that the places a bathing suit covers are very private and only a doctor, you, or her mom are to see those private places. Let your daughter know that if anyone touches her private parts to let you know about it. Don't let her run around naked at home. Talk to her about clothes before she buys them. Even if you're divorced and your ex-wife disagrees with you, stick with it for your daughter's sake. I guarantee you that in the long run, teaching your daughter modesty will make her feel better about herself.

2. *When she dates, sweep the garage.* Every boy who dates your daughter needs to know he is accountable to you. It doesn't matter if he's just taking her for coffee or taking her to the movies. It doesn't matter if he's just a "friend." Let him know you'll be waiting. And when he brings her home, be sure he sees you.

When my own daughters went on dates, my husband frequently worked on outside chores (even at night). He'd shovel snow or sweep the garage. Usually he'd start working on these chores fairly close to the time the girls were supposed to be home. He claims he didn't do this consciously. I don't believe him. Because of his night-time chores, the driveway floodlight would always be lit. No hanky-panky in our driveway!

Many parents make the mistake of trying to stay in the background. Parents fear being too controlling or overprotective. We don't want to embarrass our daughters. But daughters tell me they feel loved when dad insists on shaking hands with their boyfriends, and when he circulates among her friends at a party.

If a boyfriend picks your daughter up at home, don't let him wait in the car and honk the horn. Make him come in and see you. Before the two of them leave, ask your daughter what time she'll be home. (Of course, you'll know already, because you and she have discussed a curfew beforehand. You simply want to be sure that *he* knows when she is to be home.) Then tell her boyfriend you look forward to seeing him again at nine or ten or whatever time you set.

As a father, you may think this unnecessary. After all, you reason, your daughter is a good kid. That's exactly my point. Nice girls can be too nice. Over and over again nice girls tell me how they date boys they don't like and have sex with boys only because they don't want to hurt their feelings.

That's exactly why you need to protect your daughter from herself. Remind boys that you—not your daughter—will hold them accountable for their behavior.

3. *Plan with her.* Teach your daughter that sex is for later. Let her know that her body isn't ready—and neither are her emotions. Some fathers encourage daughters to wait until after college or after high school. Some encourage waiting until marriage. From a medical standpoint, infection risk is all about numbers of partners. The fewer she has, the better. One is best. From a psychological standpoint, the same is true. Girls who avoid deep romantic attachments during

their teen years have lower rates of emotional problems. Girls who avoid sexual activity in their teens have lower rates of depression. Let her know that the longer she waits, the better.

Many fathers give their daughters a necklace or a ring to remind them of their commitment to delay sex. I know cynics say that this doesn't work, that girls will break the pledge and then feel like failures afterward. But they're wrong. Giving your daughter a token of your esteem for her can have a powerful effect. It's a reminder of what you expect from her and how highly you value her. It will build her sense of self-worth and strength. It is a tangible pledge. Even if a ring or necklace helps your daughter wait only a year or two longer, that's a victory. The longer a girl waits, the fewer lifetime sexual partners she has. The fewer the partners, the less likely she is to get an infection.

Hattie came to my office several years ago for a physical. She was sixteen and life was pretty good, she said. I asked her if she had a boyfriend. She quickly and emphatically replied no. I wondered why a sixteen-year-old would be so adamant. So I asked.

"No, it's not that I don't like boys, it's just that I've got a lot of stuff on my mind. And when I have a boyfriend, I start doing things I really don't want to do."

My curiosity rose.

"Like what?" I asked her.

She seemed startled at first and then said, "Well, see my ring?" She held out her right fourth finger. "My dad gave it to me three years ago before he and my mom got divorced. I don't get to see him much since he's in South Carolina. Anyway, I almost got into trouble once, and this really helped me."

She continued, "Last year I was dating a really nice guy. He's a year older than me. We went out for a few months and we talked about sex and stuff. He didn't know what this ring was all about and I didn't want to tell him 'cause it's special between my dad and me. Well, one night we were out late and you know, we, um, started having sex. I really wanted to. So, we kept going. Then when I moved my hand up, I saw the ring. I felt weird. I felt guilty and confused. I wanted to keep going. But I thought of my dad when I saw the ring and I stopped. I really did." Her tone was insistent.

"I believe you, Hattie."

And as easily as she told me the story, she changed the subject and was off onto another.

Don't let anyone tell you—or her—that it's impossible to wait. It absolutely can be done. Make it something you expect of her. And if you want to, give her a ring or a necklace as a reminder.

4. *Say something*. Fathers squirm at the idea of discussing sex with their daughters. Make it easy on yourself by keeping it simple and starting such discussions in the fourth or fifth grade, when most public schools start their sex education programs. Just as you discuss the rest of her school day, talk about this and find out what they're teaching her. If you disagree with what she's being taught, correct it. Tell her to come to you for answers to her questions.

As she gets into junior high, ask her what her friends are doing. Ask what other kids, even the ones she doesn't like, are doing. Are they drinking? Are they having sex? Let her know your views. Continue these conversations through high school. Watch her behavior, how she talks to kids on the phone, how she dresses, where she goes. If she's acting seductive, there's probably a good reason why. Say something.

Most important, let her know your dreams about her future—her safe, happy, healthy future. Talk to her in private, when you're both relaxed. Car trips are great, even bedtime. Many high school girls tell me they love to have their dads come in and say good night. It makes them feel loved and safe. And the influence can be lifelong.

Mary, now forty-two years old, is the mother of four children. She told me that from the time she can remember until she graduated from college, her father came to her bedroom every night to say good night.

Her father, Brett, was a general practitioner in a small town, and Mary remembers their phone ringing constantly. He would routinely leave during the night to help anyone who was sick. Her mother waited long hours in the evening to have supper with him. Mary said that she missed him terribly but deep down admired his commitment to a job he felt was noble. He cared deeply for his patients. But Mary always knew that he loved her and his family.

"I guess that's why his coming to say good night was so special," she told me. "I didn't see my dad as much as I wanted and those few minutes we spent together were private. They were just ours."

Mary went on to say, "I would just be dozing off when light from the hallway would appear in my room. He would pad over to my bed and sit on the edge. He was big and the side would droop, causing me to roll toward him.

"Sometimes he sat there and we'd talk. Other times if I was too tired I sensed him praying. He never prayed out loud, just in his head. He told me he thanked God for me and that I was special. Then he always leaned over to kiss me before leaving and whispered words in my ear that I thought at the time were peculiar. He'd say, 'Remember, Mary, your wedding night. It's very special and so are you.' That was it.

"You can't believe how good that made me feel about myself and about my dad. When I was in high school and college I met guys and wondered if they felt like my dad did. If they didn't, I brushed them off. Dad was a giant in my eyes. What did I do about sex in high school and college? I can tell you that I thought long and hard. And every time I thought about it I heard his words. They never made me feel guilty or bad. They made me feel strong and in charge of myself. And because of them I turned a lot of guys away who wanted sex."

◈ ◈ ◈

This is the protection that you alone can give your daughter. It will pull her closer to you. It will give her a sense of authority over her body, her sexuality, and her life. No television actor, pop star, or magazine can give her that. You can. While they pull her toward promiscuity, you must stop them dead in their tracks.

Let me put it this way. If you don't want your daughter to be sexually active in high school, you need to tell her, you need to teach her. Otherwise, she will be. Popular culture trains our daughters for a life of promiscuity.

Every model for *Playboy* is someone's daughter. Don't let it be yours. Protect her beautiful body as only you can. She may hate it in the short term, but when she is an adult she will thank you. And the thanks will come sooner than you think. Stay in the battle.

Chapter Six

❖

Pragmatism and Grit:
Two of Your Greatest Assets

Kelly is on my A-list of incredibly cute patients. She is ten. Freckles plaster her face. And she has bright, fuzzy red hair. But Kelly's cutest quality is that she bounces. Everything about her bounces: her inflections, her demeanor, her movements.

Her father and mother, Mike and Leslie, are excellent parents: calm, engaging, enthusiastic, and good disciplinarians. When their son (now college-age) was little, they decided they wanted to add a daughter to the family by adopting a girl. They chose Kelly.

However, Kelly is often a tough kid to parent. She is strong-willed and challenges everything Mike and Leslie say. When they correct her, she insists that they don't understand—and sometimes they think she's right.

Kelly is one of those kids who began showing signs of hyper-activity while still in diapers. She wasn't as much defiant as energetic and testy. At school her energy was channeled into her tongue and her heart. She talked to friends constantly, often dis-rupted class, and was a problem for her teachers. On car rides she talked nonstop. When she was happy, her parents were happy. But as Kelly grew older, she grew testier—so much so that Mike often didn't even want to be around his own daughter.

One afternoon Mike and Leslie came to my office to talk about Kelly. They hold professional jobs and were immaculately dressed. When I asked, "How are things at home?" Leslie erupted in tears. Mike sat quietly.

"Out of control," Leslie said through her tears. "Something's wrong with Kelly. We can't get through to her; she argues with us all the time. Just about every interaction Mike or I have with her is negative."

Mike nodded his head. "She's right. Whenever she acts out we take something away from her, and now we have nothing left to take away. She earned a horse, which we rent for her, and I guess we could take that away, but that's her only outlet for exercise and relaxation."

"What have I done wrong?" Leslie cried. "We've tried everything we can. Is she acting this way because she resents us, because I work, because she is adopted? I don't get it. We never had this problem with her brother. I know we parent slightly differently because they are different kids, but come on, should we see a psychiatrist, a counselor? Do you think she has learning problems? Could she have bipolar disorder? Why is our home so tense? Please—tell me where we went wrong."

Mike watched his wife. His love and concern for Kelly was palpable and he felt equally sorry for Leslie.

Leslie talked for about forty-five minutes while Mike and I listened. She cried; we waited. He nodded in agreement and occasionally offered a comment or two.

Finally he said something that irritated Leslie: "So, Dr. Meeker, what can we do?"

"You don't understand, do you?" blurted Leslie. "We need to *understand* what's wrong. Where have we let her down? Why doesn't she love us?"

Leslie took Kelly's behavior extremely personally. She wanted to know why Kelly felt the way she did, to empathize and understand. This is often how women engage problems.

Mike, it was clear, approached the issue differently. I watched him—outlined in his neatly pressed suit, crisp white shirt, and navy tie—as he calculated, reasoned, and figured his way through the problem. He was looking for a solution. While Leslie assumed personal responsibility for Kelly's problems, Mike didn't. The problem was just there and had to be solved. Leslie approached the problem with intense feelings. Mike's response was pragmatic.

"What can we do?" he repeated.

At that moment the three of us fell silent. I must admit that, as a woman, I felt for Kelly and empathized with Leslie's emotional response. But as we sat quietly, I realized that Mike had the wiser approach. I made a list. I drew clear lines and separated Kelly's behavior—she had been diagnosed with attention deficit hyperactivity disorder (ADHD)—from her person.

"Leslie," I said, "because of her ADHD, Kelly is wired differently; her motor is running furiously, and she can't control it. Neither you nor Mike gave her that motor; it's just there. You and Mike have been great parents, but you can't change her wiring."

She seemed relieved for a moment. I continued.

"You know I don't believe in over-medicating kids with ADHD, but Kelly is someone whose ADHD is severe enough that she could benefit from a small dose of medication. I think you'd see an enormous result."

"I know, Dr. Meeker, but Mike and I don't like stimulants. I just really think that we can help her lick this."

I tried a different tack. "Leslie, let's say that this is your fault. Your ten-year-old girl is hyperactive, a compulsive talker, and a strong-willed child because you are a bad parent. Could that be true?"

Mike looked up at me with horror. I thought he was going to jump up and choke me.

Leslie, stunned, nodded her head. "Yeah, down deep that's what I believe. I just screwed up."

"Mike, do you believe you're a bad father?"

"No, absolutely not. I've tried my best. I love Kelly. She's just who she is."

Mike and Leslie were churchgoers and actively involved in mission work, so I recruited the image of God for help. "Okay, Leslie, I know you believe in God. What about Him? He's a perfect father, isn't He? Isn't that what you believe?" I asked.

"Yeah," she answered.

"Well, look at all the messed-up kids He has."

I think then it dawned on Leslie that even God, the perfect father, had children who misbehaved terribly.

My friend Bonnie—a nurse practitioner, licensed clown, and Episcopal deacon—had made this comment to me several years ago after she found out that her own adopted daughter had become pregnant at age seventeen. Bonnie wanted to start what she called "the worst mothers in America" club. Then, she said, God reminded her that He, too, had a bunch of rebellious children.

Mike reasoned that Kelly needed structure and routine peppered with fun—and that she needed the medication I recommended. While Leslie continued to worry, Mike opted for action, and we agreed to put Kelly on medication.

A month later, Leslie called and said Kelly was doing great— even felt better about herself. She laughed, she felt in control, and she wasn't getting into trouble at school. Leslie and Mike enjoyed being with her again.

My point is that fathers are often the ones who bring pragmatism and solutions to family discussions. Men see problems differently than women do. Women analyze and want to understand; men want to solve—they want to *do* something. This often annoys wives and daughters, who can get swept up in thoughts and emotions, and conclude, as Leslie did, that you "just don't get it, do you?" or even that you're uncaring or heartless. But that's only because you're less interested in talking about a problem than in doing something about it.

For more than twenty years I have watched fathers come to grips with their daughters' problems, analyze them (sometimes in an almost mechanical way), and solve them. Of course, I'm not saying that all fathers are analytical or pragmatic or better at this than their wives, but it is certainly true in general that mothers and fathers have complementary approaches to problems: fathers reach immediately for solutions while mothers yearn to understand and empathize. Your daughter needs you to be that voice of reason and pragmatism.

Why Your Daughter Needs Your Pragmatism

A girlfriend of mine quipped that there are two types of women in the world: princesses and pioneer women. Princesses believe they deserve a better life and expect others to serve them. Pioneer women expect that any improvement in their lives will come through their own hard work; they are in charge of their own happiness. To most of us, princesses are spoiled—but whenever we teach our daughters that they deserve "all the best that life has to offer," we help to create princesses. But princesses are often depressed, because they might not ever get the best that life has to offer. Princesses are taught to be self-centered. Their lives are centered on their needs and wants, and they will expect others—parents, teachers, friends, and eventually spouses—to focus on meeting these needs and wants. Princesses use the pronoun "I" so often that their lives become narrow. And their search for the best that life has to offer is hopeless, because there will always be something better just out of reach. We groan at the neighbor's child who screams "I want!" all the time, but is she any different from the twenty-five-year-old professional who consistently draws conversations back to herself and who thinks of other people as objects to be manipulated for her own ends?

Girls think and feel and wonder about their thoughts and feelings. And because many girls (probably your own daughter) are equipped with the psychological finesse to figure out how they feel and what they want, they are naturally gifted at figuring out how to get what they want.

But here's where dad comes in. When your daughter daydreams about the sort of girl she wants to be and what she should expect from life, she takes her cues from you. If you teach your daughter—even inadvertently—that other people exist to serve her needs and desires, she will grow to expect that from others. If you teach her that life has limits and that not all her needs or desires can or should be met, she will learn to accept realism, and she will not live expecting—or waiting for—others to be servants to the princess.

Your daughter's attitude toward herself comes directly from you. Her expectations, her ambitions, and her assessment of her own capabilities all come from what you believe—what you say and what you do. As a father, you have to ask yourself what sort of woman you want your daughter to become.

Every doting father of a four-year-old girl wants her to be his princess. We dress girls up, lavish attention on them, and unabashedly melt when they say "I love you." Even at fourteen or twenty-four, daughters secure an inviolate corner of their fathers' hearts that is theirs and theirs alone. A daughter's needs are foremost in dad's mind. Her ambitions become dad's goals. All of this is wonderful and healthy. But be careful.

The damage comes when a loving father indulges a daughter to the point that she expects always to be on the receiving end, and that all her material, physical, or emotional needs are to be taken care of by someone else. What or how much you give her doesn't matter as much as the way in which you give. I have seen many wealthy girls grow up unspoiled and many poor girls become demanding, selfish grown-ups.

The trick is to teach her that gifts, love, and attention are wonderful, but that she is not the center of the world. You want to teach her to appreciate these things and be humbly thankful for them. You do not want her to feel entitled to and selfishly focused on them.

Princesses take. Princesses want more. Princesses demand. They expect perfection and lack pragmatism. They don't act—except to tell others what they want.

But pioneer women know that life is the way it is, and they rely on themselves to move forward.

As a dad, whenever your daughter is in a tough situation, all you have to do is ask her this simple question: "So what can *you* do about it?" And it's worth asking that question in situations throughout her life.

Inevitably, your daughter will encounter pain. People die and loved ones get cancer. She might not get asked to the prom. She might get pregnant at sixteen. She might develop an eating disorder. She will encounter problems, like you did. Some can be solved, some cannot. But if she is to live a substantive, healthy life, she needs to decide what to do about her problems. Princesses encounter problems too, of course, but they expect others to solve them. When princesses get bad grades, or get pregnant at sixteen, or get kicked out of high school, it's always because someone else messed up; it's always someone else's fault. They expect others— usually those closest to them, especially dad and mom—to play an inordinate role in correcting their problems.

Don't let your daughter grow up to be a victim of life. Too much of our popular culture teaches us to love victims. So we create people who are helpless, incapable, and terribly needy. But you, as a father, can prevent that. You can teach your daughter that she needs to *do*, not just to *want*.

Action helps; action can cure. And dads are experts at analyzing a problem and finding something to do. The action your daughter takes can be anything from making friends, changing schools, or even thinking differently. Action engages the will and gives energy and momentum. Action means that your daughter will know that she, not others, will determine her fate.

I have seen many young women with eating disorders. They cannot begin to recover until they commit themselves to working hard at a programmatic cure. This is true with depression, alcoholism, and many other conditions. As a doctor, I diagnose problems, devise a plan of treatment, and then give instructions to patients. In very much the same way, a dad is a physician to his daughter.

Let me show you how Bill helped Cara with anorexia nervosa. When Cara was eighteen, she came to me—on her own—because she was feeling sad, confused, and dizzy. Worse, her fingers and toes were turning blue. She had no idea that she had an eating disorder. Her brain was so starved that her thoughts had become tangled, almost delusional.

I diagnosed severe anorexia nervosa. She was near requiring hospitalization. Her heart had slowed, her hair was falling out, and her circulation was so poor that she was literally growing cold (hence the blue fingers and toes).

Her parents, Bill and Cheryl, were terrified. Cheryl cried a lot; Bill stayed quiet. At home he threatened Cara if she didn't eat. He took days off work to stay with her and force her to eat. Cheryl screamed at Bill for treating Cara this way, and Cara fought with her mother because her dad was so mean. Life at home was tense, unhappy, and depressing.

After a few visits with Cara, I spoke with Cheryl and Bill. He did most of the talking, because Cheryl was in tears. Cheryl couldn't get past why Cara starved herself, what caused her starvation, or what she and Bill had done to precipitate Cara's anorexia.

Bill said that he couldn't begin to understand. He was a wreck. He had said that neither threatening Cara nor rewarding her helped her to eat. They were at the end of their rope.

But Bill wanted a plan. He didn't want the whole plan. He just wanted the first couple of steps to get started.

Cara went to a residential treatment home and was immediately placed on a very rigid eating schedule. If she didn't follow it, the tube went up her nose and nutrition was pumped through it all night long. She was taught about anorexia nervosa. Counselors helped her examine her feelings. They asked her to discuss how she related to her parents and friends.

Cara's counselors always asked her, "What can you do today to talk back to the monster in your head?"

Treating anorexia nervosa often requires interrupting and changing or replacing the ugly, denigrating thoughts inside the sufferer's mind. It is a continuous, repetitive process: interrupt thoughts, replace them; interrupt them again, find what triggered them, then replace them. With a problem like anorexia nervosa, as with a multitude of other problems girls encounter, understanding isn't enough. Each girl must be challenged to act. She can't wait for others, feel sorry for herself, and wallow in the pain of life. In order to find her way out, she must do something.

Frustrated as wives can be with husbands who are program-driven, goal-oriented, and task-solving, men have these qualities for a reason. It is a father's programs, goals, and actions that can make the difference in solving a daughter's problems.

Teach Her to Use Grit

When we think of masculine men, we (women at least) envision those with one overriding quality: a spine of steel. Nothing makes a woman's heart melt like a man with courage and resolve. We admire men who are willing to risk their lives to help good triumph over evil and who have the moral wit to distinguish between the two. Masculinity means strength. You see it in the way men work. Men in construction start their jobs early and end them late. Soldiers in Iraq risk their lives every day. Pilots continue to fly in spite of personal fear. Men in high finance are often highly charged, deeply driven, and propel themselves through hard work to success. Men work with such intensity because they have grit. Sometimes you can have so much grit, so much hard-driving, so much silent internalizing of frustration and stress that it can kill you.

But that's in the workplace. Now think about your home life. Here is your place of quiet and solace: a friendly family dog and a doting wife and children. Don't you wish?

Home is work too, because just as people need you to do things at work, your wife and your daughters need you to do things at home. Not just fixing things around the house, but being the man they need you to be. That can sometimes mean intervening in their disputes and helping them solve their problems.

Pragmatism helps men find solutions to problems, and grit enables you to apply these solutions day after day, year after year. These two qualities teach your daughters how to do the same.

❖ ❖ ❖

After the first two months of first grade, Doug noticed that Gretchen's enthusiasm about school was waning. She stopped wanting to practice her reading. She cried when she went off to school in the morning. He scheduled a time to meet with her teacher. "She's a lovely girl," her teacher informed him. "I just don't understand. She does excellent work in class." Doug was dumbfounded.

Whenever he talked to Gretchen about school, she said she hated it. She didn't like her teacher. Her teacher was mean. She made kids read out loud whether they wanted to or not, and she wouldn't let kids go to the bathroom when they needed to. Doug thought that these were problems, but not serious ones that would make a kid not want to go to school. His wife, Julie, worried that something bigger was going on. "Maybe she's depressed, maybe she has dyslexia or someone is humiliating her at school," she told Doug. She wanted to take her to a psychiatrist. They argued about what to do. What exactly was the problem? Was it school, was it the teacher, was it a bully in her class, or was she struggling with ADHD or depression? They went to the Internet. Julie became convinced Gretchen was depressed and needed help, maybe even medication.

Doug decided to do some detective work. Periodically, during his lunch hour, he would go to Gretchen's school and walk past her classroom. He listened to what was going on inside. Sure enough, he heard her teacher tell one student to shut up and yell at another to sit down and be quiet, "or else."

He went to the principal and complained. Julie went to the teacher and scolded her for treating the children badly. The teacher stayed on and her behavior didn't change. Apparently other parents had complained too, to no effect. Julie wanted to send Gretchen to another school. Gretchen wanted to leave.

But Doug told Julie he wanted to try something else first. Give him six weeks, he said. She relented. Doug informed Gretchen that he would take her to school from now on: she wasn't going to take the bus anymore. She liked that. "I wanted a little more time with her before she left for school," he said, but I think he had more up his sleeve.

On their car rides, they talked. "Honey," Doug said, "you have one really bad teacher in your class. I'm sorry. It must be frustrating and scary."

"It's horrible, Daddy. I don't know why you make me keep going! Mommy says I don't have to. Take me home, I don't want to go school," Gretchen would say.

Morning after morning their conversations continued along these lines. Doug was the voice of realism and accepting that life can't always be perfect. Yes, the teacher had no business teaching first grade. Yes, she had a temper and she said things that she shouldn't say, but, he told Gretchen, you can handle it. "She's a mean lady," he agreed, "but you need to think about what you can do to make going to school and attending her class better."

At first Gretchen wouldn't answer him when he said that. But gently, over the next few weeks, he kept telling Gretchen that it was up to her to improve things in class. Finally, she began coming up with ideas. "I could raise my hand less, Daddy, but do you think that would make her mad?"

"Or," she continued, "Mom and me could make fun lunches every day. And maybe I could go to resource room during math!" Gretchen and Doug schemed. They thought of serious things and silly things. Gretchen had fun just coming up with ideas.

Here's the point. While Julie wanted to yank Gretchen from the classroom and spare her the hardship, Doug wanted to teach her that she could deal with it. He wanted her to know that, in tough situations, there are many things that won't change. He told her it was unrealistic to expect that her teacher would stop yelling or be nicer. But there are always things that she can do to make things better. He wanted her—even as young as the first grade—to understand the famous prayer "God grant me the serenity to accept the things I cannot change, the courage to change the things I can, and the wisdom to know the difference." Gretchen did just that.

Did she like first grade? No. But she developed character. She learned how to stay in a tough spot and act, and not just be a passive victim. Did her father tell her, coldly, to just shut up, stop complaining, and behave? No. He listened to her, he sized up the situation, and agreed with how she felt. He told her that she was right to feel upset. But then he helped her find solutions. They worked together, and little Gretchen learned how to not just endure but to thrive during a difficult time. Sure, it would have been easier if Gretchen had simply switched schools. But Doug took the extra time and extra work to build Gretchen's character because he knew it was what she needed.

❖ ❖ ❖

Many of you men who are extraordinary at performing, thinking, and reasoning at work come home exhausted, and all the skills you practice every day on the job evaporate once you get there. While grit keeps you moving forward at work, at home you may become a pushover or simply disengaged. Dads, you must have grit at home too. Home life requires just as much tenacious engagement as work does. So consciously spare some energy at work.

I am convinced that if fathers recruited even 20 percent of the intellectual, physical, mental, and even emotional energy they spend at work and applied it to their relationships at home, we would live in an entirely different country. I'm not referring to coming home and doing more chores around the house, the yard, or at your kids' schools. I'm talking about truly engaging with your family as a husband and father. Much of what you can do for your daughter is simply to engage her in conversation and listen. Men often talk little, but they listen more. Your problem-solving brain can analyze what your daughter tells you, and you can help her think of ways to smooth over volatile situations.

Nowhere is your masculine strength and manly grit more needed than at home. The greatest difficulties, joys, and pains of life aren't at your job, they're with your family. Your masculinity either shines or loses its luster at home, and what you do there can be the difference between keeping a loving family together and watching it drift apart or crumble. You can't maintain a good relationship with your wife or daughters if you're never home. You can't maintain a good relationship with your wife or daughters unless you're there for them. I know you might not want to, but this is where you need to show your grit. You need to stay and listen and navigate female frustrations and hostility. We—daughters, mothers, and wives—need you to stay, to bring your courageous, goal-oriented reason that provides solutions.

Some of you dads might find yourselves right in the middle of a conflict between your daughter and your wife. When women argue, emotions fly, doors slam, and conversations can become venomous. And you feel torn between your love for your wife and your love for your daughter. But in such conflicts, fathers are often the perfect arbiters, putting emotion aside and being the voice of reason. I know it's not always easy to do that. Some situations are complex and fraught with volatile feelings.

For example, when a mother dies or leaves home and a father is left to raise his daughters alone, he has difficulty figuring out what to do and what to say in the normal challenges of everyday life. But more difficult is the challenge to help his daughter grieve for the loss of her mother while he grieves for the loss of his marriage. If you eventually remarry, the stresses on your relationships can be redoubled. Stepmother troubles with daughters are particularly common. While every father has within him the tools necessary to handle such stressful situations, here are a few things to remember.

First, remember that you and your daughter were together before you and your new wife. In your daughter's eyes, she has more right to you than your new wife does. If she feels her relationship with you is threatened, she will take her anger out on your new wife. So be very careful. Give your daughter all the time she needs to adjust before you bring a new woman into your home. Remember that your daughter needs you more than your new wife does. You are your daughter's lifeline; you are not your wife's lifeline. When your daughter is an adult, your allegiance can shift to your wife. But at least until she is twenty-one, your daughter's needs have to come first. I know this is tough advice, but if you follow it, your life will be simpler and easier, and you can end up with a happy daughter and a good new marriage.

Second, let your daughter grieve. Sometimes men become so pragmatic that they forget to feel, and forget that others need to work through emotions. Grieving for the loss of her mother is a very healthy and important process for a daughter. Simply telling your fourteen-year-old to buck up and get on with life four months after her mother is gone is cruel—and it won't help. In fact, it will make your daughter disconnect from you and become angry and bitter. One of the biggest problems girls encounter after a mother dies or leaves the family is ungrieved loss, especially if their father later falls in love with another woman. It is natural for your daughter to feel angry about her loss, to feel mad at God for allowing it, and even bitter that you didn't stop her mother from leaving or dying. She can, for a while, feel angry and bitter about everything and everyone. This is completely healthy and normal. Once this passes, she will begin to come to grips with the profound sadness she feels inside. She will cry, perhaps withdraw for a time, or become sullen. Her emotions can become tangled as she feels anger and sadness at the same time. Finally, she will come to accept that life is the way it is, and, if you have helped her along the way, she will feel hope. She will begin to be able to look forward to a new life.

But here's what frequently happens when a new wife or girlfriend appears on the scene. Your daughter's grieving process is interrupted. This can be devastating to girls—they can feel betrayed. And, honestly, some girls simply can't deal with a new woman around, at least not without the passage of time and the assurance that they still come first with you. If you want to remarry and have a successful family life, you simply must give your daughter time to complete her grieving. Otherwise, your daughter might never get along with your second wife.

Third, remember that she's the kid and your new wife is the adult. Ask more from your new wife than from your daughter. Your new wife should be able to handle it (and if she can't, find that out before you marry her, because it's a warning sign). It is common for daughters to feel jealous of a new wife, even common for them to have a strong and irrational dislike of everything about her. Your new wife can inadvertently feed these feelings.

Some new wives want no trace of your first wife around. They want to be the center of the family and don't want to be compared to your first wife. They feel threatened and insecure. So, a bit of advice, not only for your daughter, but for you: if your girlfriend can't be comfortable talking about and accepting your first wife as the mother of your daughter, you should end the relationship. If you don't, it could tear your family apart.

Many men become so wrapped up in their own grief that they choose to marry or date women they never would have chosen in any other situation. So please give yourself time to grieve and adjust, and only then think about new romance. This is just as important for your potential second wife as for you and your daughter.

❖ ❖ ❖

Theresa was an only child. Her parents adored her. When Theresa was in the second grade, her mother was diagnosed with a very aggressive form of breast cancer. In spite of chemotherapy, surgery, and radiation, she deteriorated rapidly. Within a year, Theresa's mother was dead. Theresa was nine years old. She sat at her mother's funeral cold, pale, and rigid. Her father, Brad, was in so much grief that he sought help from friends and from a counselor. He took Theresa to a grief counselor too. He did this for six months, and it didn't seem to help. The counselor told him that

Theresa was unresponsive and that Brad was wasting his money on the sessions.

Theresa went to school, came home, went to her room, and shut the door. There, on her pink bedspread, she cried hour after hour. She spoke infrequently to her father. And she never spoke about her mother. She even took her mother's pictures down, which upset Brad.

Within twelve months of her mother's death, Brad began dating a new woman. Since Theresa rarely spoke to him, Brad was desperate for company. He hadn't known this woman, Helen, before his wife died. She was organized, comforting, and brought a sense of normalcy back into his life. Whenever she came to the house, Theresa glared at her and refused to speak. After three short months of dating, the two married and Helen moved into the house. Brad and Helen both believed that once they got married and Theresa got used to Helen, she would come around and talk. She would be happy because she had a woman in the house to care for her.

Theresa made it through grade school, junior high, and the early high school years fairly well. She never seemed really happy, but at least she could be cordial to Helen and her father. Besides, she said, her father demanded that she be courteous to Helen. This was the way life was now, he told her, and she just had to accept it. He had needs too, he let her know, and he could help her a lot more as a father if he were happy.

But Helen struggled. She had her own two children, who were grown. She talked to them every day on the phone. She wasn't as pretty as Theresa's mother had been, and she was uncomfortable with Brad talking about things he and his first wife had done together. She silenced talk about his first wife, and even when Theresa referred to her mother, Helen reminded her that that life was over. She was there now. She was the new woman in the home. She wanted to be spoken to with respect and she wanted Theresa to understand that it was good for Brad to be shared between the two of them. Helen was hotheaded, and as Theresa grew into her teen years, she lost her temper with her. She called her names and swore at her. Theresa came to hate her stepmother. She told her father what Helen would say to her in his absence. Brad tried to tell Helen that she needed to get along with Theresa, but Helen responded by berating him for having such a disrespectful daughter. The house became an emotional minefield. Finally, during her junior year in high school, Theresa ran away. She hated her stepmother and swore she would never come home as long as Helen was there.

Brad handled this terrible situation with determination, pragmatism, and grit. First, he recognized that even though Theresa looked like a grown woman, drove a car, held a part-time job, and paid some bills, she was still, in some ways, a crying grade-schooler who missed her mother; she had never completed her grief at losing her. Brad realized that Theresa had needed more time than he had given her. So he began spending more time with her. Even though she wouldn't come home, he met her at a friend's house, they met for coffee, they even went away once for a weekend. He gave himself back to Theresa. Helen fought him. She demanded that whenever Brad was with Theresa, she should go along because Theresa needed to accept her.

Brad didn't abandon his wife, but he politely insisted on having time alone with Theresa. Helen was furious, but Brad told her that was the way things were going to be. She had to deal with it because she was a grown-up and Theresa was a kid. Many insecure second wives refuse to let a husband spend time alone with his children from the previous marriage. Fathers, don't let this happen. You need to be strong, like Brad, because your children really do need time alone with you.

Slowly, Theresa began warming up to her father. Interestingly, he said, the closer she got to him, the more agitated she seemed sometimes. She had never acted that way before and he was confused. His counselor told him that this was a good sign. Theresa was more comfortable with him, and that meant more comfortable in sharing her emotions. She felt closer to him emotionally, she felt more secure, and she no longer feared he would abandon her (as her mother's death had made her feel abandoned) if she opened up about her feelings. For two years they talked about her mother; they cried and they argued, and they talked about things the three of them had done together. During this process, Brad noticed that Theresa's grades improved. She eventually started coming over to the house for dinner. And three months before she graduated from high school, she moved back home. She never really warmed up to Helen, but that was all right, she said. She felt that she had her dad back. Brad even apologized to Theresa for marrying so quickly. He was bereft, he told her. He had felt crazy with grief and he couldn't think straight. Theresa forgave him.

Brad did it right. Did he make a lot of mistakes? Sure. He made tons of them, but that didn't really matter because he did the big stuff right. Today he has a terrific relationship with both Theresa and Helen. But that didn't come easily. What did he do right?

He initiated restoration with his daughter. Not content to sit by and watch her grow darker and more embittered by the day, he engaged Theresa in the midst of her difficulties. He figured out what she needed, and he did it for her. He allowed himself to see the world from her perspective. Was she a bad kid who hated the world and everything in it? Well, he said, it sure appeared that way. But he knew deep down that she wasn't. She was a very sad little girl who repeatedly got pushed aside.

I watched Helen and Theresa get so entrenched in passionate anger and frustration that at times they couldn't speak. Their feelings literally overwhelmed and incapacitated them at times. Brad, on the other hand, while he loved both of these women, seemed to look at the whole picture from a broader perspective. His vantage point was: "Now, today, what can I do? What should I do next to smooth things over?" He stood back from his wife and daughter, made a practical plan (with the help of a good counselor), and then, day after day, argument after argument, he stuck to it. He was pragmatic, he was determined, and he pursued his goal with masculine grit. He did things right not just for himself, but also for the two women he loved. And, because of how he handled a terrible situation, everyone won. He saved his relationship first with his daughter, then with his wife.

Keep Your Family Together

I have observed relationships between fathers and daughters, husbands and wives, and mothers and daughters for more than twenty years. I have poked and prodded patients; I have listened and learned about ailments mental and physical; I have given antidepressants and on occasion have even asked people to leave my office. When I graduated from medical school in the early 1980s, I took an oath to stay committed to ensuring the health of my patients.

Medicine has made enormous scientific advancements that allow me to see inside my patients' bodies so clearly that it's like looking at a drawing in a textbook. I can give medicines that calm kids down, cure some cancers, and extend the lives of kids who have HIV.

But all the tricks in my medicine bag cannot ensure that my patients will live a successful life. I can usually keep them alive to adulthood, but then many collapse. Daughters become confused by cold boyfriends. They enter relationships unable to trust men—or trust them too much. Many young men are terrified to marry because of what they have seen—or not seen—at home growing up.

Fathers, you can make the difference. And one huge way you can make a difference is by keeping your family together. The most common cause of unhappiness and despair, what crushes the spirit of children more often than anything else, is divorce. Divorce is really the central problem that has created a generation of young adults who are at higher risk for chaotic relationships, sexually transmitted diseases, and confusion about life's purpose. But that's where fathers who stay engaged with their families can make all the difference.

But suppose it's too late. Suppose you are already divorced. If that's the case, move forward, and use all the grit you have to reshape and improve your relationship with your daughter. If you haven't been front and center in her life, commit to it now.

Think about it this way: If you lost your job, would you give up working? Of course you wouldn't. You couldn't afford to. You can't afford to lose your daughter either. If you've lost your relationship with her, devote yourself to retrieving it. You can do it. Masculinity embraces difficulty as another problem to solve. I know that many men lose hope in their relationships with women, because women confuse them. I have watched this occur over and over. But this is exactly why men—life's pragmatists—must be encouraged to stand back from the complexities of relationships and simplify life. Prudence often requires waiting. It requires the masculinity of strength, self-control, and the grit to stay involved.

Ranting quiets itself. Anger burns out. Hearts break and then return to life. People mature. And if you are the rock your daughter can cling to, she can overcome every challenge of growing up.

❖ ❖ ❖

Alex and Mary had three daughters. Mary experienced serious, and worsening, postpartum depression after the birth of each child. Alex didn't handle Mary's depression very well, he admitted, and frequently worried that she might not recover after each episode. She would lie in bed for days, crying, unable to come out of her room. He hired help for her. He took days off from work. He did whatever he could to keep the family going. They both did. In fact, by the time their girls entered high school, their relationship felt solid again. Mary never experienced any more major depressive episodes after her third pregnancy.

When their daughter Ada turned fifteen, Alex noted that she began wearing darker clothes. Ada was the youngest of the three girls; Ellie was seventeen and Alyssa was twenty. Ada switched friends at school. She attended an art school for talented musicians and was an outstanding flutist. But she began to ignore her friends and started dating a seventeen-year-old high school dropout who occasionally worked pickup jobs.

Alex was stunned. Within six months, Ada had gone from a concert-level flutist who enjoyed being at home with her parents in the evening to a girl who refused to play her flute, study, or stay home when she was told. Alex scaled back his hours at work and spent more time with Ada. He picked her up from school occasionally and took her to lunch. He took her to movies. He checked on her at night (to make sure she was still in bed). Once he took her to Chicago for the weekend.

All of this wasn't hard for him, he said, because he genuinely loved Ada. He felt sorry for her. They had had a good (though not extraordinarily close) relationship up until that time. Alex and Mary felt guilty that they had somehow failed her as parents. Mary feared that her postpartum depression had maimed Ada emotionally.

When Ada was sixteen and a half, she ran away. Alex was devastated. He hired a private detective to find her. Ada had stolen money from her parents, gotten on a bus and then a train, and had found her way to San Diego, far from her home in the Midwest.

Alex left for San Diego to bring Ada home. He found her working behind a cash register at a convenience store attached to a gas station. For a while he just watched her interact with the customers. Suddenly, they locked glances. He waited until she had a break, then they went outside. Ada screamed at her father through her long, charcoal-black hair. She refused to come home. She had found a "friend" with whom she shared an apartment. (Alex later found out that her "friend" was a divorced thirty-year-old man.) For three days Alex reasoned with her, cried, and pleaded with her to come home. Ada refused. "If you force me home," she said, "I'll just run away again."

Alex came home without Ada. His heart was broken. He felt he had failed as a father, though he didn't know how, and he couldn't understand why Ada hated him and her mother so much. All she would say is that she had wanted to leave. One year to the day—a year without letters or phone calls—Alex returned to San Diego. He found Ada working part-time at a car wash. She looked ill and numb. Again, for three days he cajoled, pleaded, and cried. She refused to budge. Even though she had been kicked out of her apartment and separated from her roommate (for reasons she refused to divulge), she preferred shelters to her home with Alex and Mary.

Another year passed. On Ada's eighteenth birthday, Alex—feeling like his heart had been ripped from his chest—returned to San Diego. This time he found her living on the streets. He barely recognized her, and feared she had become a prostitute. She denied it, and he believed her, though he assumed she must be taking and dealing drugs. After three more days, Ada still wouldn't leave with him. He gave her new clothes and returned home.

This pattern continued until Ada reached her early twenties. Alex wrote her letters, but never sent them, as she didn't have an address. He saved money for her in a savings account. He told no one about this, fearing they would think him a fool.

But he loved her and he wouldn't stop. Ada had sliced his heart into thousands of pieces but he was determined to love her. He couldn't change her but he could love her.

One October day, his cell phone rang while he was at a board meeting for a local bank. "Daddy?" came Ada's voice. Alex couldn't speak. His brain became hot.

"Daddy, are you there? Please talk." She began to sob.

"Ada, where are you?" he finally choked out.

"I'm in Grand Rapids at the train station. Daddy..." She began to cry and could no longer speak.

"Don't move. Ada, don't move. Please," he pleaded.

Alex excused himself from the meeting and raced down the highway to get Ada. When he saw her, she was emaciated and she had shaved her head bald. She wasn't dirty, but she looked very old. He ran to her, grabbed her, and engulfed her in his arms. He could feel her body tremble as she sobbed. He walked her to his car and drove home. They sat silently. But slowly things got better.

Ada stayed home, got a job at a local gas station, and at twenty-three, finished high school and began taking some local college courses. She even began playing her flute again.

At first, Alex told me, he was so relieved that his elation kept him company. Then, he said, something terrible began to happen. Anger churned inside him. He was disgusted with Ada. The healthier she became, the more he disliked her. He had nightmares of fighting her physically. When he found her arguing with Mary, Alex wanted to choke her.

He was confused and threw himself harder into his work. He never showed his anger to Mary or Ada. He kept it inside, and the worry ate at him. Sometimes, he said, his anger was so intense he feared he might hurt someone.

But he didn't. Alex kept his cool, even as every day became a struggle just to get out of bed, go to work, and keep it all together. The toughest times, he said, were at home. He would see Ada, and he could hardly bear it. Some days she was nice. Some days she flew off the handle. She never said she was sorry. She blamed her behavior on drugs. She said she had started taking drugs in high school and they had made her into another person.

Ada matured, moved out of the house, and eventually got married. She never finished college, but her revived musical skill landed her a job with an orchestra, and she blossomed.

As a young married adult, Ada now lives a couple of hours away from her parents. She calls Alex weekly on his cell phone. She talks to her mother too—but not like she talks to Alex. She asks his advice, tells him she loves him, asks him to visit, and is hurt if he can't. No one ever figured out why Ada did what she did. There was no understanding it; it just happened. But it was only Alex's tenacity and grit that brought her back—even as he suffered silent rages—until she put her life back together. Alex and Mary are still married and, after years of trial, happily so.

Alex's behavior reminded me of five lines from Tennyson's poem "Ulysses":

> We are not now that strength which in old days
> Moved earth and heaven; that which we are, we are;
> One equal temper of heroic hearts,
> Made weak by time and fate, but strong in will
> To strive, to seek, to find, and not to yield.

In saving Ada and his marriage, did medicine, psychotherapy, faith, and friends help Alex? Yes, they all helped in part. But ultimately, Alex restored his family because he refused to relinquish his daughter. He determined how to help her and then he steeled his will to do it, because that's what strong fathers do.

Chapter Seven

⟡

Be the Man You Want
Her to Marry

Get ready. One day you and your daughter will be standing at the back of a church, temple, or garden. Your arms will be linked. You will be looking down the aisle, past rows of people, at a very nervous young man.

Your daughter's arm shivers against yours.

You whisper to her, "It's not too late, you know."

"I know, Dad. I'm okay."

You swallow hard and wonder, *How did my little girl get here so fast?*

Here's another sobering thought: the man you see at the other end of the aisle will undoubtedly be a reflection of you—be that good or bad. It's the way it is: women are drawn to what they know.

That prospect might terrify you. If you have had a tumultuous relationship with your daughter, if it's been filled with cold distances, intense arguments, or chronic misunderstandings, you might well worry. But keep reading—because from a daughter's perspective, it's never too late for the two of you to improve your relationship, to break the terrible cycle, to change for the better.

Back to this tuxedo-clad fellow. If you could pick his personality, what would he be like? You would want a young man totally committed and faithful to your daughter. You would want him to be hardworking, compassionate, honest, and courageous. You would want a man who will protect your daughter. You would want a man of integrity.

Before your daughter marries, you need to be that man. You need to ask yourself: Do I live my life as a father with integrity? Am I honest? Do I work hard for her and my family? Am I loving and protective of my wife and daughter? These are very tough questions, but if you want a healthy marriage for your daughter, this is where it begins. A healthy marriage is based on respect. You want to have your daughter's respect, and if you model integrity, you will—and you will teach her to expect it in her future husband. Choosing a spouse is one of the most important of life's decisions. Careers don't bear children, fill you with exuberance, or bring you soup in bed. Spouses do. And you are the man who will teach your daughter about men.

See It, Do It, Teach It

Allow me to let you in on a frightening secret about physicians. While we are in residency training to be specialists, we work horrific hours. A typical week includes eighty to ninety hours of work in the hospital, often more. Under pressure, we learn to do procedures quickly.

We are taught: "See one, do one, teach one." It can be anything from placing an IV to doing a lumbar puncture to intubating a comatose patient. Once we are shown how to do a procedure, we are expected to do it, and to teach another physician-in-training how to do it.

For your daughter to know what a good man looks like, she has to know one. She has to see a model of masculinity in you. And what does that mean? It means you need to be a man of integrity— a man who inspires trust and respect, a leader. It means that you need to live with honesty, you need to live your life committed to your family, and you need to be willing to sacrifice for them.

Honesty is more than telling the truth. It means not keeping secrets. Not only does secrecy isolate people from each other, but when you're hiding something, it's rarely good. It's usually something about which you are embarrassed or ashamed. It is a weakness.

Believe it or not, deceit has risen dramatically among kids. According to one recent study, 76 percent of public high school students (out of a survey of 18,000 students at 61 schools) admitted to cheating on exams.[1] The same study, "Smart & Good High Schools" by Thomas Lickona, Ph.D., and Matthew Davidson, Ph.D., cites data showing a steady increase in cheating over the last few decades. In 1969, for instance, 34 percent of students admitted to using a cheat sheet during a test. In 1989, that number rose to 68 percent. One student wrote that students have to cheat because if they don't, they'll lose to kids who do. But excuses don't matter. What matters is the erosion of integrity in kids.

Honesty sits at the heart of integrity, and we have done a bad job of teaching honesty to young people. I see this in my practice, especially with kids who become drug users. It's a process. They start keeping secrets from their parents, telling lies, sneaking peeks at pornography (especially on the Internet), dabbling in alcohol (maybe from dad's liquor cabinet), and then trying out marijuana with friends "just to see what it's like." Marijuana is a "gateway

drug," leading to harder drug use, including cocaine or metham-
phetamines. I don't need to tell parents about what drug use can
do to kids.

Parents know intuitively that one bad decision can lead to
another; small problems left uncorrected can become big ones. We
adults understand this progression. Yet all too many parents are
too distracted, confused, or intimidated by politically correct
moral relativism to clarify right and wrong behavior for their kids.
So many kids opt for lying and cheating because it's easy and
appears—on the surface—to make them more successful.

Don't let this happen in your home. Stop it before it happens. If
it has already happened, confront it and implement a plan to
reverse it.

And as you confront secrecy and dishonesty, you need to be a
model of integrity and strength, of honesty and openness. You
need to be a leader for your family. Your wife and daughter need
a strong man, not a weak one. And a strong man knows that nothing good ever comes from secrets; nothing good comes from iso-
lating yourself from your wife and daughter; nothing good comes
from giving in to temptations to lie, or abuse alcohol, or view
pornography.

I know you are bombarded constantly with sexual imagery. I
have a husband and a son, and I know the temptations they face.
Sexualized advertising has done tremendous harm to young girls
and women. But that harm multiplies threefold for men. Sexual
imagery grabs your attention in a way that it doesn't for most
women. It's not that women aren't interested in sex, but visual
stimulation is very different for men than it is for women.

Every day, you are seduced. On your laptop at the office or the
television screen in your hotel room, women of all shapes and sizes
lure you into secrecy. And the problem is, secrecy may feel innocu-

ous and titillating at first, but the patterns established can be devastating. Pornography crushes your masculinity but seems as though it enhances it. It lies to you repeatedly, pulling you into deeper isolation, deeper weakness.

It's up to you to be strong, to realize that your family needs you back. Your daughter, your son, and your wife need you to live without the secrets—about pornography or anything else. Truth heals, and truth sits at the core of integrity.

Amber, now twenty-six, told me a story about her father that beautifully illustrates the point. When Amber was fifteen, she remembers awakening in the middle of the night to her parents screaming. "My mom and dad rarely argued," she told me, "and I couldn't understand what they were arguing about. But Mom was angrier than my father. Apparently she had found out something he was doing. She was crying and raging.

"My mom had been sick for a year with a lymphoma, and then from the chemotherapy and radiation she needed to cure it. I felt so badly for her. We all tried hard to help her. My younger sister and I cooked. And we kept quiet in the afternoons while she tried to nap.

"My dad was wonderful too. He tried to help as much as he could but his work was a bit overwhelming. Plus"—she became teary as she continued—"he was having a hard time accepting my mom's illness. He loved her so much. I think he was terrified about what would happen if she died."

Amber's emotions were intense, and as she continued, she spoke louder and faster.

"Anyway, that night they were arguing, and I got out of bed and went downstairs. She must have found my dad at his computer and she freaked. I assume he was looking at something, writing to someone, I'm not sure. I didn't really want to know—this was my dad."

Amber quieted and her tone softened. "Over the next few months they cried a lot and argued off and on. They didn't tell me or my sister exactly what was going on at the time, but finally my father sat all of us down one day and did something I'll never forget. My sister and I were on the couch facing my father and my mother—who was bald from her chemotherapy and radiation. He did all the talking.

"'Girls,' he said, 'you know that Mom and I have been having some problems.' When he said these words I felt like I was going to vomit. I was sure he was going to tell us they were getting a divorce.

"He had a hard time talking. We waited. I became incredibly nervous. Finally he said, 'Here's the problem. Me. I haven't done a very good job handling Mom's illness. I'm really sorry for you girls and for your mom. I don't expect you to understand, and Mom and I aren't going to give you details because that's between her and me. Anyway, I've made some terrible mistakes. I'm taking our desktop out of the house. Since we all share it, this means that you'll have to tell your friends no more e-mails or IMs.' Then he looked at us, clearly worried about what we would say.

"'That's it?' I asked him. 'You and Mom aren't getting a divorce?'

"'No, Amber, no divorce. Mom needs us: you, your sister, and me. This is really, really hard right now, but we've got to do the best we can to stick together. I know how hard this is for you too.'

"That was it," she said, still obviously surprised at how little he explained. "He sat there, sad and quiet. We all stared at each other. After a little while my sister and I went up to our room totally confused about what was going on but relieved that they weren't getting a divorce.

"I wish I could say everything after that was fine. Now it is, but for about the next year, my folks really struggled. Mom got better and they began talking more.

"After eavesdropping on their conversations, my sister and I figured out what was going on. Apparently my dad got into a relationship with some other woman on the Internet. It didn't go on terribly long and I don't know if he even met her. I think I know when all of it started. Anyway, I'm sure one thing led to another and he got into other stuff too."

Clearly, Amber didn't want to say the word *pornography* because no one wants to connect their own dad with sex.

"But here's the cool part," she said. "After that day, I heard my mom and dad talk about having no secrets from each other. And as best as I can tell, they never did again. The computer hit the bin, and over the past few years they have become happy again."

Amber communicated her pride in her parents, particularly in her father, as we finished our conversation. Without making excuses for him, she realized that the electronic, unreal world of the Internet seduced him when he was weak from grieving. He tried to keep this unreal life secret because he knew it was wrong. In the process, his family began to crumble around him.

"But," Amber said, "he got it. He realized that it didn't work. It all got exposed and it was at that point that my dad started to turn things around. And you can't believe how good it feels that he did." Amber isn't married yet, but she has a serious boyfriend whom she very well might marry. What do you suppose she will expect from him? Will she close her eyes to secretive behavior—or will she expect him to rid any secrecy from his own life, as her father did? Because Amber's father had the courage to face his hidden life and change it, she will expect the same from other men, or think less of them. Amber's father not only changed his own life, but he also changed hers, drawing them much closer together. Her father probably never realized it when he made his announcement from the couch, but his decision had an enormous impact on Amber's future and on her future happiness.

The Internet can be a friend because it can enable you to work from home, on vacation, wherever. But it can also be your biggest nightmare. Treat it fearfully. Pornography is so addictive to men and young boys that it snakes its way into your life without warning. It is more addictive than alcohol, easier to access than drugs, but equally destructive to men, wives, and children as either of these two. Dr. Lickona writes, "Pornography can fry your conscience and you won't even notice." Men of integrity notice everything, particularly things that threaten their welfare and the welfare of those around them. If you let your daughter and son know that pornography is a struggle for every man and boy, and show them that it can be dealt with and avoided, you will give them unmatched power to confront the hard things in life. And I can guarantee that you improve your chances that your daughter will insist on the same in her future spouse.

Every father wants a son-in-law who has nothing to hide and whose relationship with his daughter will be founded on truth. All secrets hurt. So talk to your wife about this. Make an agreement to have no secrets between you. Practice this. Then watch what happens to your daughter. If you live a life without secrets, she probably will too. If you expect her to hide nothing, she is much more likely to come clean about drinking and other dangerous behavior. But if she finds out that you (or her mom) are living with serious secrets—and kids almost always find out—she will likely do the same.

If you have to go solo on your commitment to "no secrecy,
it. Lead. Face your weaknesses and find ways to avoid temptations. If your weakness is alcohol, give up drinking with your
friends and spend more time sober with your family. If your weakness is women, set rules to protect yourself. Billy Graham (even he,
a spiritual giant of our age) felt tempted by other women, so he
always took a male friend with him when he traveled so that he
would never be alone with a woman. His rule might not be yours.
You decide. How much is your daughter worth to you? If you hide
things, so will her husband. You need to put your family first. And
that means before your career as well.

Concerning lying, talk about the importance of truth to your
daughter. Teach her to expect it from others and help her to be
savvy at recognizing it in others. (She will have plenty of opportunity at school.) Tell her that you and she cannot have a meaningful
relationship if lying sits anywhere inside it. Why? Because even if
either of you lies "just a little on occasion," then trust breaks down
between you. Let your daughter know that you want a relationship
with her based on trust; that alone will draw her closer to you.

You also need to take a hard look at your own thinking, speech,
and behavior. This is tough, but you must do it. Your daughter
watches you all the time, and the truth is, if you're lying about
something, she may not know the details, but you can be certain
that she knows something's up. Daughters are like that. My husband and I were friends with another couple for many years. I'll
call them Bob and Hilary. They visited our home frequently, spent
weekends with us, and so on. They were fun to be around and we
laughed a lot together. They seemed very happy in their marriage.
One day my husband received a phone call from Bob. Bob was
beside himself with anger and grief. He found out after twenty-two

...hat his wife had been having a pretty serious ...We were shocked. Unfortunately, my husband ...ng this in the kitchen one night. Two of our daughters, then aged ten and twelve, overheard us. They walked into the conversation and we had to tell them, flat out, what had happened. I will never forget what our oldest daughter said: "Mom, Dad, that doesn't surprise me one bit. Something about Aunt Hilary always bothered me. She was kind of creepy."

As easily as she entered the conversation, she exited. She "knew" something all along. Don't think you can hide secrets. Older kids have a way of knowing or finding out.

Good Men Are Hard to Find

Men with integrity stay truthful. But finding an honest man can be hard in today's moral climate. Think about the statistic that 76 percent of public high schoolers have cheated on exams. If your daughter goes to a typical public school, chances are the boy she's dating is a cheater and a liar. (And the odds are also high, higher than 40 percent, that he's had sex and will lie to you about that.) Well, you say, if he's just cheating on exams, that's not so bad; she's not going to marry him anyway. Maybe. But she is starting to establish patterns of dating and communicating with men, and if she learns to expect that boyfriends naturally lie, and that she has to accept that, her standards will be lower than you want them to be.

❖ ❖ ❖

Six years ago one of my former patients, Alicia, went to the West Coast to a very prestigious university. She graduated with honors and took an excellent job with a marketing firm, following in her father's steps, in New England. While living there, she met a man, Jack, who was five years older. She fell madly in love with him. They dated for six months and she wanted him to meet her father, so she and Jack went home for a long weekend. While they were there, her father and Jack talked casually and both seemed cordial, but they weren't connecting the way Alicia had hoped. On the third day of the visit, Jack announced that he had to leave early because a family problem had come up. So he left and a few days later rejoined Alicia in New England.

After the visit, Jack and Alicia decided to move in together. He wanted to let go of his apartment, and Alicia was thrilled because she felt marriage was imminent. So Jack moved into her apartment. The next three months were happy and smooth. He worked as a lawyer or a paralegal, she really couldn't understand which, she said. Apparently he had gone to law school but didn't pass the bar exam and was going to retry in the future. In the meantime, he worked at the firm and held other jobs here and there to supplement their income. Finally, he asked her to marry him and she was elated. She called home to tell her folks and they received the news poorly. She called her best friend and her response was similar. In fact, her dad drove to her apartment for the weekend after she told him.

"Alicia," her father said that weekend, "you can't marry Jack. Something's not right. I don't trust him." While her father couldn't put his finger on exactly what was wrong, he said what he felt. Alicia became so upset with her father that she asked him to leave her apartment. After all, she said, she was a fully mature twenty-five-year-old woman. If she had to choose between her future husband and her dad, she would choose her husband.

They planned the wedding, and her relationship with her father was cool at best. He continued, respectfully, asking her not to marry Jack. But the wedding was imminent. She had sent out beautiful wedding invitations to four hundred guests. She had had pictures taken. She had paid the band and the caterer. The bill for the floral arrangements alone was $8,500.

Two weeks before the wedding, Alicia received an anonymous phone call. She didn't recognize the voice on the other end. Jack was watching television in the living room. The person on the phone was a woman who said Alicia was making a big mistake and should get out of the relationship right away. Alicia couldn't speak. The woman only said that Alicia wasn't "the only one." Alicia hung up the phone and didn't know what to do. At first she blamed her father for putting someone up to the call. But then she realized that her father would never have anyone call and lie to her. Surely, she thought, the anonymous caller was lying about the other women. She couldn't call her best friend, because they had grown apart. She didn't want to call her father, because she felt humiliated. So the next day, feeling sick to her stomach, Alicia called a private investigator. Within twenty-four hours, the private investigator found out that Jack had four other names. He had three wives, had never been to law school, and was currently working as a runner at a law firm. He had two children by different women, and there was a warrant out for his arrest in another state for embezzling money from a law firm. Somewhere along the way, he had had documents forged claiming that he had a degree from a very respected law school and that he had passed the bar exam.

There was only one place for Alicia to turn. She made the phone call. "Dad," she cried quietly. "Can you come up right away? I mean, can you come up tonight?"

"Sure, honey, but what in the world's wrong? Are you sick? Do you need money? Did someone hurt you?" He was startled.

Alicia's father jumped in the car and drove to her apartment to find her standing outside. She was shaking. She wouldn't go inside because Jack was there. When she saw her father, she did what every girl in trouble who has a good relationship with her father does. She began to sob. She had held it all together, but the minute she saw him get out of the car she fell apart. He hugged her and she shook for the next five minutes, barely able to speak.

"It's Jack, Dad. You were right. He's a creep and a crook." She handed him the investigator's report.

"Well, there's only one thing to do now."

"What?"

"Go confront Jack with this. Kick him out. Call the police. Do whatever we need to do to get him as far away from you as we can."

"Dad, no! No! What if he shoots us or something?" She felt out of her mind with fear.

"Look, honey. I'm going to deal with him. Do you want to come with me, or should I go in alone?" he insisted.

The two went in to see Jack. No one got shot. Alicia's dad stayed with her for the next few days and changed the locks on her doors. After he felt that she was safe, he went home.

"The amazing thing was," Alicia told me one year later, "that he never ever rubbed it in my face. He never said 'I told you so,' or anything like that. He just came and helped me take care of things. It was devastating. But I have to tell you I was scared. Do you know what it's like to live with someone that closely and never have a clue that they have another whole life—or two or three?"

But here's the best part about what she said that day. "You know, even while my dad was warning me during that time, something really bothered me about Jack: he was so different from my dad. Of course I didn't want to tell anyone. I mean, he talked differently and I caught him in a few white lies. My dad never did that. My father was quiet and honest. It never dawned on me that I couldn't trust him, but I wasn't ever quite sure whether or not I could trust Jack. I thought, how can I live with that? In my mind, everything Jack did I compared against my dad. I knew, I knew, deep in my heart that I could never marry someone so different from my dad, but I don't know, I guess I was just totally blinded by infatuation. How could I have been so stupid?"

I wonder if Alicia realizes that the man she is currently dating is very much like her father.

❖ ❖ ❖

Alicia's story is extraordinary to me, not just as her doctor, but as a mother of grown daughters. This is one sharp young woman. She is confident, highly respected at work, and has a lot of integrity. So what went wrong? She was blinded by love and, more important, she failed to listen to her father.

Jack's deceit nearly ruined her life. Lying hurts. Hiding things hurts. People's lives are better if they live with honesty and integrity. And if you live that way in your work and in your life, your daughter will benefit.

People Come First

Men, of course, are trained from the day they enter school to be career-oriented, and most men measure their career success and even their happiness in terms of money. We all like to believe that having more will make us happier. So many men think in terms of gain: material things, career advancement, a bigger bank account, a prettier wife. But the constant pursuit of more never leads to happiness; it only leads to dissatisfaction with what we have.

When we realize that we don't *need* more, then we can relax and be happy. Contentment comes with being satisfied with who we are and what we have today. A man who lives his life with integrity will have that sense of contentment and freedom. His example will teach his daughter an important lesson about life's priorities. But if you don't reconcile your wants and desires with honesty, integrity, and humility, your daughter won't either—and nor will the man she chooses to marry.

Do you want your daughter to marry a man who believes that the life he has with her is not enough? His feelings might be disguised as driven perfectionism, but it will mean that he will always be looking for more. He will start looking away from her, their children, and their home life in order to find fulfillment. He will hurt your daughter. As a father, you don't want to put your daughter second to a search for more. But if she sees you constantly striving for more—and I mean beyond working hard and doing a good job—she will expect that the pursuit of more is necessary to have a better life. If you teach her, by example, that happiness requires a bigger house, a higher salary, more cars, a boat, and expensive vacations, she will marry a man who constantly leaves home to do the same. People who are dissatisfied with their material possessions can become dissatisfied with who they are—and who other people are. After your driven son-in-law gets the other stuff he wants, he might want more from a wife: perhaps a smarter, quieter, more assertive, or more attractive wife. It doesn't matter what he looks for in another woman, because it could be anything.

Don't set your daughter up for that pain. Show her the truth that the most important part of our lives is our relationship with loved ones. Those relationships are the only avenue for deep joy and contentment. When they are good, life is good, and we feel that we need little else. That's what you want your son-in-law to feel—and if you model that behavior, your daughter will seek a husband who does the same.

It's a great strength to live knowing that if you lost every material possession, you would still have a life worth living. That means living without fear. We live frightened of things being taken away, but we don't need to be afraid. Strong relationships ground us. They complete us. You don't have to worry about losing material things; your life won't collapse without them. You can treat them as gifts and focus on the loving relationships that are really important, for they are the greatest gifts.

If you live this way, your daughter will perceive that she, too, is a gift. You might even tell her that on occasion. She is a gift who has changed your life through her love, compassion, and strength. Teach her that she is enough. She needs to know this so that when she chooses a husband, she will look for another man who considers her a gift, who considers her "enough." Living with "nothing to hide, nothing to gain, and nothing to lose," as author Ken Davis puts it, is real freedom. You want your daughter to live freely, without fear. So show her how. Be the man you want her to marry because chances are excellent that when she is mature, she will look for you (albeit subconsciously) in another man. If you haven't a clue what a good father looks like, look around and find someone who is doing it well. Then watch him, learn from him, mimic him. As you practice, you will change your daughter's life. She will absorb who you are. And one day, she will turn around and reward you with a son-in-law you can respect.

Finding Balance for Yourself—and for Her

Wise fathers know that the difference in their daughters' lives between exhilaration and disaster, joyful contentment and erosive anxiety, can turn on a single smart or foolish decision. Your three-year-old daughter runs her scooter into the street. Your fourteen-year-old breaks from the group at the theater and heads off alone with her boyfriend. Your nineteen-year-old drives home from a party after just a "few" drinks.

As a father you have to live with this tension. You want to keep her safe, but you want her to be independent. You want her to be bold but not careless. You want her to love but not to be too needy. While you cannot change her personality or determine all the challenges in her life, you can support her, point her in the right direction, and help her mature. And how your daughter matures will depend on what she sees when she watches you wrestle with the big issues of life, when you show courage amid challenges. Where can she see your courage exercised at home? Everywhere. My sister-in-law watched her physician father go into prisons to perform autopsies on people who had died of AIDS when no other doctor would. I recently heard a father of fifteen-year-old twin girls tell them that they could be okay, even happy again, after their mother died of breast cancer. I saw anguish in his eyes but heard conviction in his voice.

Your marriage might not be everything you want it to be, but it takes courage to keep it together and to put the needs of your children ahead of what you might—often mistakenly—think would be your own happiness. Courageous men take stock and do what is right. Integrity is not complete without humility. True humility comes from finding that balance between who you are and what the world is. And the great reward is that humble fathers are wonderful to be around. Daughters love humble dads and distance themselves from haughty ones.

Humility and balance also play a role in knowing the difference between healthy love and suffocating love. You will want to protect her. She needs you to fight for her and to care, to be there for her, to be strong. She wants the world to know that if you mess with her, you mess with her dad. Don't let her down. Fathers who shrug their shoulders and turn away leave their daughters feeling crushed.

❖ ❖ ❖

I know Allison's father quite well. He is a mild-mannered, successful lawyer who tries hard to be a good father. They have a home by Lake Michigan, where Allison frequently threw bonfire parties at the beach. During her senior year in high school, they had a party that her father welcomed as a way to meet the kids in his daughter's class. He also believed, as many fathers do, that teens need their space. So after the fire was lit on the beach, he and his wife stayed away and never checked on the kids. They didn't want to embarrass Allison. They suspected that some of the kids were drinking alcohol, but assumed they couldn't get into much trouble on the beach.

The fire died down and kids started to leave. One young man got into his car to drive a few friends home. He was the designated driver and, although he'd had a few drinks, he hadn't drunk as much as the other kids. On the way home, his car slid out of control and two of the kids in the car were killed. His life, the lives of the dead kids' parents, and Allison's parents' lives were never the same. They were sued and Allison went to jail—all because her father didn't want to embarrass her. Fathers, you need to interfere.

Listen to your instincts and err on the side of protecting your daughter. It is a common mistake of fathers to back away from their daughters too fast and too soon. Please, please don't. You're not being overprotective or overbearing if you keep her from learning the hard way that drinking too much is dangerous, even life-threatening. Protect her, but do so subtly and wisely. Be there. Be the man of integrity, with reason and with muscles, to keep her pointed in the right direction.

Recently I spoke with a father (a single dad named Mike) who had just returned from a trip to Mexico. Like many parents, he was worried about senior year spring break. So he took his daughter and some of her eighteen-year-old friends on spring break as his guests. After two nights at the resort, the girls decided, of course, that they wanted to experience the nightlife and asked if they could go to a local dance club for a few hours. Not wanting to seem prudish or "untrusting," he said they could. He laid a few ground rules. First, they had to stay together. Second, they couldn't leave the club. Third, only two drinks apiece. Fourth, they had to leave for home at 11:30 p.m. This was their test and he let them know that.

After dinner, the girls primped and took a taxi into town. Mike took a taxi fifteen minutes behind them. Cautiously, he strolled the narrow streets outside, peeking into the club every once in a while. He waited and he walked. At 11:30 he walked back to the taxi area. No girls. At 11:45 he became concerned and peered into the bar. There they were—all four of them, laughing loudly, with rosy cheeks. His daughter was conversing with a bearded man of about thirty. "What time does the last cab run to the resort?" he asked a cab driver.

"Twelve, no later," was the response. Fifteen minutes and they would have no ride home. Did they get it? At 11:55 he walked up to the bar and tapped his daughter on the shoulder. When she turned around she was furious. "Do you know what time it is?" he asked her.

"We're coming, we're coming," she giggled. "Dad, sorry. You know I don't wear a watch."

She collected her friends and the five of them caught the very last cab out of town back to the resort.

"I was seeing red!" Mike told me. "I was so mad, so disappointed that I had to wait until the morning to talk to them.

"So I waited until after breakfast and we were all sitting on the beach. I asked them how the night was. 'Fabulous, Mr. Trent,' one of them said. My daughter stayed quiet. She knew I was upset.

" 'Did you stick to two drinks?' I asked. They all nodded yes. 'What time did we leave? Does anybody know?'

" 'Yeah, about eleven-thirty, just like you asked us, Mr. Trent.'

" 'See, Dad, we were fine!' Lizzie said. 'I was sooooo embarrassed when you came in, Dad. Why did you have to do that?' she said.

" 'Liz, anyone,' I asked, 'do you know what time the last taxi left town?'

"They looked at me with blank stares. Silence.

" 'It left at midnight. Midnight. What time did I yank you from the bar?' I asked.

"Again, blank stares.

" 'Eleven-thirty?' one girl asked.

" 'Nope. Eleven fifty-five.' They said nothing. 'What would you have done if you had missed the last taxi?'

" 'Dad,' Liz said. 'We met these *really nice* guys in there. They're from the States. One's name was Zach and he said he had a car. He offered to take us home with his friend.'

"I exploded. 'Are you kidding me?' I screamed. 'You were going to let a strange guy you just met in a bar drive you home?'

" 'Dad, you just don't understand. He was really nice. I mean it.' "

[Warning to all fathers: whenever your daughter says a guy is "really nice," that means he has a nice smile.]

"I think the thing that bothered me the most," Mike told me, "was that these girls really didn't get what I was saying. I couldn't convince them why they shouldn't leave bars with 'really nice' guys they just met. Plus, they completely ignored the parameters I gave them. I found out, too, that one of the girls spent the entire evening dancing and drinking with a guy who was married and vacationing at our resort with his wife and kids but told her he was single and there on business.

"They drank too much; they paid no attention to being responsible or about getting home. And the biggest mistake was that even my own daughter was ready to depend on some stranger to give her a ride. What would have happened if I hadn't followed them?"

Mike's dilemma was all too common. He knew Liz so well and even thought he knew her friends well. Liz is bright, a freshman at an Ivy League school, and never gets into trouble. What did he miss? Just this: the fact that Liz is smart, responsible, and enrolled in a good school doesn't change her brain development. She has a nineteen-year-old brain, not a twenty-five-year-old one. She walks the tightrope between fun and disaster and can't catch herself if she teeters to the wrong side. But fortunately for her, she has a dad who trusted his male instincts to protect her. By listening to those instincts, he might have saved her life.

Would Liz and her friends probably have survived the evening without disaster? Yes. But maybe they wouldn't have. Her life was too important to Mike to take that chance. And he was right not to take it. I say that as a doctor who has seen too many fathers' daughters take too many chances. Mike hit just the right balance between trusting and protecting.

The balance slips when protecting becomes micromanagement. Pediatricians use the term "hyper-parenting" when referring to parents who over-schedule their kids and micromanage them. The intentions of hyper-parents are usually good: they want their daughters to excel and seize a multitude of opportunities. The problem is that kids can feel pressured and suffocated by such parents—and they can turn bitter and unappreciative. So stay balanced, set up protective boundaries, and keep her safe, but give your daughter freedom to choose activities she enjoys, and make sure her days are filled with opportunities for downtime.

Finally, men with integrity keep their daughters in the human race. Cyber-life exists and it is not going away. But while there's no need to teach her to fear electronics and media, be smart and don't let her "unplug" from human company and center her life on cell phones, iPods, mp3 players, and BlackBerries. Balance. I have known fathers to run over iPods and mp3 players with their trucks. And I have known others who encourage their teens to go to summer computer camp for eight weeks at time. Keep your daughter engaged with you as much as possible. Go away together, out to dinner, play golf, or go fishing. Talk to her; hug her. The Internet can stir emotions in her, but it can't console her when she is crying. You can, so be there.

So what does this have to do with her husband? Everything.

He, too, needs balance in order to have a healthy marriage with her. If she learns balance from you by watching you struggle to find it on many different levels, she will want it as well. She will watch for it in any boy she dates. If she never learns what balance looks like regarding courage, love, and faith in a man, she could marry a mistake. That mistake might be a man full of bravado, with an arrogantly cold heart and a cynic's faithlessness—and he could break your daughter's heart.

Or it might be a man who "loves her so much" that he needs her to be near him always, to listen to his concerns and advise him about his relationships or his work. He finds her so wise, in fact, that he is afraid to make any decisions without her help. Maybe he is recovering from alcohol addiction or depression. She is "good for him," he tells her, and his neediness makes her feel wonderful.

Watch out, fathers. Fellows like this are all around and nice girls love them. They swoop in to care for these needy, broken-winged

pigeons, and whammo! She marries him, she gets
him until he is "strong enough" to work, and in
weight on her shoulders becomes unbearable.

Or worse, he might actually hurt her one day. The incident of
violence between boys and girls and men and women dating is terrifying for us parents. According to the National Youth Violence
Prevention Program, almost all middle and high school students
have experienced physical or emotional abuse while dating. Specifically, one in eleven middle and high school students has been hit,
slapped, or physically hurt on purpose while dating. Another one
in eleven said that they were forced to have sexual intercourse. And
an astonishing 96 percent of students report that they have experienced emotional or psychological abuse while dating. Girls are
markedly more at risk than boys in every one of these statistics.

❖ ❖ ❖

Tara went to a small southern parochial college. She was excited
to go because the school had an excellent program for people who
wanted to teach the blind and deaf. Several months into her freshman year, she befriended a man in her class who was on a full basketball scholarship. She had grown up in a middle-class suburb; he
was a tough inner-city kid. But he was pleasant, funny, and very
respectful to her. He told her that she was the most beautiful
woman in school. She spent hours listening to him and talking at
coffeehouses. Several times he asked her to go on "dates"—to dinner or to the movies. She declined because she wanted to keep their
relationship as a friendship. He didn't like this and became more
and more aggressive with her. Tara explained that she didn't want
a boyfriend just then; she wanted to concentrate on her studies.
Tension arose between them, but Tara felt sorry for him. He had

d a terrible life growing up. He never knew his dad, and his mother was in jail (for second-degree murder, she later learned). His siblings were alone and he worried about them constantly. He wanted to finish college and get a good job so that he could support them. Tara admired that. She did not cut off the relationship because she felt she was overreacting to his anger and agitation. "He wouldn't hurt me; he just really needs me," she thought. Ironically, she also was afraid to cut the relationship completely because of what he might do. He was big and she feared making him angrier. (Fathers, take note: many, many girls feel this way. They are afraid to break up with a boy for fear that he will harm them.) Finally, she didn't want to stop the relationship because she thought she could help change the course of his life. (Another warning for dads: this is also extremely common among nice girls. They really believe they can get men to stop drinking, yelling, being mean, and so on.)

As the school year came to a close, Tara got ready to go home for the summer. When she went to say good-bye to her friend, he was angry with her. Many of the students had left the dorms. Late in the evening while she was getting ready for bed, she heard something at her window. He was there. Her roommate was gone. He forced his way into her room and raped her. There were students next door, but he put a pillow over her mouth so that she couldn't be heard. Tara got pregnant and the next five years of her life were hell. All because she wanted to be nice to this man and help him.

❖ ❖ ❖

Alcoholics and depressives need help. But they can get that from a doctor. Your daughter needs to be protected, and you are her shield. You need to model a healthy relationship in front of her.

Show her what healthy love looks like. A love that is balanced. Then she will know what unhealthy, unbalanced love is. And if it comes into her life, she will turn away before things get out of control. But if they do get out of control, be ready to help her, like Alicia's dad was when he dealt with Jack.

If you want her to marry a man with integrity, a man who will try to love her well, a man who will exercise courage with his family, protect her, and embody manly humility rather than arrogant narcissism, then *show* her integrity. Teach her to love life more than she fears it. Show her the integrity that means you have nothing to hide. Show her the love that puts family before material possessions. Show her strength of character and she will incorporate it into her own persona.

Integrity feels good. The more she sees it, the longer she lives with it, the more she will expect it. And she'll look for it in the man she marries.

Chapter Eight

✧

Teach Her Who God Is

Your daughter needs God. And she wants you to be the one to show her who He is, what He is like, and what He thinks about her. She wants to believe that there is more to life than what she sees with her eyes and hears with her ears. She wants to know that there exists someone who is smarter, more capable, and more loving than (even) you. If you are a normal, healthy father, you should be glad that she wants to believe in someone larger, because you know all too well that many times you will fail her. You forget her recital, miss games because of business trips, or lose your temper and say painful things to her. You are just a normal, good-enough dad doing the best you can. You need to have someone behind you, someone your daughter can turn to when you're not there. You both need a bigger, better father on your side.

I don't make statements like these lightly. I make them as a doctor, based on what I have observed, studied, and know from experience, and I make them as someone who relies on the evidence of scientific studies with reproducible facts and correlations. When I write prescriptions for my patients, for example, I need to know they are going to work. If I prescribe Zithromax for pneumonia, I need to know that there is a strong probability that the antibiotic will cure the infection. I can't say to a patient, "Good luck. I hope this works, but I can't really be sure." The American Academy of Pediatrics would toss me out on my ear.

So if I make a statement about what is good for kids, I need research to show me. That's exactly what I will show you. When it comes to our kids—what is good for them and what they want—most parents have been duped by the media to believe many things that are blatantly false, especially about religion. The media often treat religion—especially denominational Christianity—as repressive, antiquated, unrealistic, unintelligent, and maybe even psychologically harmful to kids. That is what the media say; the statistical evidence says something very different. I would like you to read the following data with an open mind. We adults all have prejudices about what kids want and need. Here's what the evidence says.

Religion is protective for kids. Studies on adolescents reproduce this fact with extraordinary consistency. Religion is defined here as a belief in God and an active participation in worshipping at church or temple, going to youth groups, and being involved in religious activities. Research shows that religion (some studies refer to "religiosity" and I am inferring it to be equal to religion)

- helps kids stay away from drugs[1]
- helps keep kids away from sexual activity[2]
- helps keep kids away from smoking[3]
- gives kids moral guidance[4]
- gives them feelings of mental and psychological security[5]
- contributes to their growing maturity as they pass from childhood through adolescence[6]

- helps them set boundaries and stay out of trouble[7]
- helps teens keep a good perspective on life[8]
- helps teens feel good and be happy[9]
- helps most teens get through their problems and troubles[10]
- helps kids feel better about their bodies and physical appearance[11]
- helps girls delay the onset of sexual activity[12]
- helps girls be less rebellious[13]
- makes girls less likely to exhibit bad tempers[14]
- make girls less likely to cut class[15]
- makes girls more likely to watch movies with a lower rating (G or PG)[16]
- protects girls from watching X-rated pornographic movies and videos[17]
- makes girls less likely to spend a lot of time playing video games[18]
- makes girls more likely to get higher grades[19]
- makes girls less likely to have depressive symptoms[20]
- positively affects personal adjustment into adult population[21]

Other studies, focused mainly on adults, but with implications for kids as well, found that religion

- may cut the chance of committing suicide fourfold[22]
- predicted suicide rates more effectively than any other factor, including unemployment[23]
- leads to higher ego strength[24]
- helps reduce paranoia[25]
- helps reduce anxiety[26]
- helps reduce insecurity[27]

These aren't just ideas, hopes, or pie-in-the-sky wishes—they are facts. Many of these findings come from the excellent studies recently released in *Soul Searching: The Religious and Spiritual Lives of American Teenagers* by Christian Smith, which I highly recommend. It is an eye-opening study on our kids' desires and beliefs. Interestingly, girls tend to be somewhat more religious than boys, and both sexes want more religion than we are giving them.

Many parents say they don't want to push God on their daughter because she needs to make up her own mind about religion. Of course she does, but that's not the point. Parents teach their children not to smoke, or drop out of school, or drive too fast. We teach our children to be respectful and kind. We teach our kids what we believe they should know about math, great literature, science, and history. When something is important, we teach it to our kids. But we back out when it comes to teaching them about God. In part, I believe, this is because many of us weren't schooled in religion ourselves; we simply don't know enough about God and faith to say anything.

But this isn't about us; it's about our kids and what they need. You need to tell your daughter what you think and believe. What you believe will have a strong impact on what she believes. And if you feel you need to start your faith journey right alongside her, do it. She'll love it.

Clarification is in order. When I say your daughter needs God, I am being specific to the Judeo-Christian tradition, which is the tradition of more than two-thirds of American teens (52 percent are Protestant, 23 percent are Catholic, and 1.5 percent are Jewish).[28] As far as belief in God goes, 84 percent of kids between the ages of thirteen and seventeen say they are believers, 12 percent are unsure, and only 3 percent say that they do not believe in God.[29]

This is consistent with my experience with my own patients and with the teens I come in contact with across the nation. Many kids may talk a lot about whether God exists, but very few are atheists. As Christian Smith states, "Contrary to many popular assumptions and stereotypes, the character of teenage religiosity in the United States is extraordinarily conventional...the vast majority of U.S. teens are not alienated or rebellious when it comes to religious involvement."[30] The fact is, your daughter is eager to hear what you think about God—and chances are she will embrace your beliefs.

Kids are born with an inherent sense that life is more than what they see. When I ask kids about their spiritual lives, they know exactly what I'm talking about. They realize that they are flesh and bones, that they read and play piano, but somehow they see in themselves an invisible, real, and wonderful part that is indefinable. There is a space in each that is the soul, and even very young kids understand this: the unknown dimension, deep, unexplored, and difficult to define or articulate. Believing that they have a soul makes girls feel good. It makes them feel significant and connected to the eternal. And you, as her father, can see this as well.

A Father's Wisdom

Can you remember sitting on the edge of your three-year-old daughter's bed, watching her bundled in the peace of sleep? You gently leaned over her to kiss her forehead and pulled the blankets around her shoulders. No father can adequately articulate the experience of watching his sleeping child—it must be lived. Now, imagine you are walking out of her room. Could you turn around and look at her and believe that the sum of her existence rests in a mass of cells?

Certainly not. But this is exactly how a rank secularist is obliged to view his daughter. She is nothing more than a genetic product of his and her mother's DNA. The puffing of air through her tiny chest keeps her alive. Your time with her is precious, meaningful, but purely a biological phenomenon. Her thoughts and feelings can be traced to neuronal firing in her brain. One day you will die and she will die and that will be that. Life began through the splitting and rejoining of DNA and when they stopped functioning, she did too.

I can't imagine a father feeling this way about his daughter. When you look at your sleeping daughter, you are confronted with a spiritual reality that you can't deny. From the moment she was born, you sensed the awesomeness of her life, the fact that there is something mysterious and transcendent about it, that she goes beyond you and your spouse. A man can banter with his friends and colleagues about whether God exists. But a father looks at his daughter and knows. Often I find parents (particularly fathers) shy away from discussing spiritual issues with their daughters. Talking about faith is akin to talking about sex. We feel paralyzed. We choke. We don't know where to start. Or perhaps we're afraid because we don't have all the answers. Perhaps we struggle with faith. That's fine. You don't have to provide all the answers, and you can keep it simple.

Kids always want to know about God. Their questions are intuitive. If you don't give guidance to your daughter, she'll come up with answers of her own—which means your authority will be replaced by someone else's. This is how cults are formed. You wouldn't ask your daughter to cook coq au vin for dinner without giving her a recipe. And God is more important than dinner.

Whether you're a Christian, a Jew, or a Hindu, when your daughter asks about God, you need to give her something to work with. Your daughter wants to hear something from you. And for most parents, that means imparting your own faith in God, which you learned, if nowhere else, while watching your baby daughter sleep.

Why God?

Why does your daughter need you to enlarge her faith in and understanding of God? Well, Carl Jung wrote that "Among my patients in the second half of life...there has not been one whose problem in the last resort was not that of finding a religious outlook on life. It is safe to say that every one of them fell ill because he had lost that which the living religions of every age have given their followers and none of them really healed who did not regain his religious outlook." Or to put it simply, your daughter needs God for two reasons: she needs help and she needs hope. God gives help and He promises her that the future will be better.

No matter how influential you are in your profession, how wealthy or hardworking, you can only offer your daughter so much. Many men don't like to face this fact. But you can't protect your daughter from all pain and suffering. When people are really hurt, they cry out to God. The reaction is natural and instinctive. I see it all the time. But when your daughter faces these situations, will she be ready? Will she know who God is? Will she know God hears her? Or will she look outward and see nothingness? Secular fathers who deprive their daughters of God often say they do so because their daughters don't need a crutch; God, they say, is only for the weak.

But every daughter needs help—and so do fathers. Don't deprive your daughter of this help and hope. There are moments when she will need it, when she will feel alone, when the only one she can turn to is God. I've sat with patients as they die, and I can tell you that death is shrouded in mystery. I held a premature one-and-a-half-pound baby boy for forty-five minutes after I couldn't resuscitate him. I have stroked the swollen feet of a comatose old woman and felt her body change as she died. These weren't physiological changes. Her heart rate stayed regular. Her breathing was rhythmically shallow. But something changed: she left before she died.

When I spoke with Judy about her memories of her car accident, her coma, and her recovery, I asked her if there was anyone she knew before the accident that she recognized as the same person after the accident.

Her answer hit me like an electric shock. "Yes. Only one person. God. Before my accident, I prayed a lot. I went to church and I got to know who God was and what Christ is all about. When I was in my coma, I felt his presence. He was there. He was right there with me. And when I woke up I only knew God at first. Everyone else in my life seemed completely different."

One of the things I like most about medicine is that it requires honesty. Sick people shoot straight. I've noticed that people who are critically ill simplify their thinking, prioritize their lives, and easily consider God. Most believe in Him. Some turn away. But kids universally believe. For some reason, the supernatural doesn't frighten them. Their hearts and minds are less dull than ours and they accept God's presence and love much more readily than we do.

❖ ❖ ❖

When Jada was eleven, she was diagnosed with a rare brain tumor. Her parents and older brother were devastated. She was strong, athletic, and appeared extremely healthy. But when her face became erratically contorted and her body shook from seizures, they knew something was terribly wrong. Jada's father was a quiet, kind man who turned his grief inward to appear strong for his wife and son. But every day after her diagnosis, he felt his guts rotting inside him.

Stu and Joaquin didn't have faith in God. They simply lived life as though He didn't exist. They never went to church. Sundays were family days. As her death grew closer, Jada began worrying about her parents. She worried about her dog and her friends. Mostly she worried about herself. At times she became visibly frightened, particularly by the process of death.

One evening, after spending most of the day in bed, Jada fell asleep for the night. But she was restless, awoke in the night, and was unable to go back to sleep.

In the morning, she walked out of her room and found her mother and father sitting in the kitchen talking. The words that came from her lips changed their lives.

"Mom. Dad. You don't need to worry about me anymore. An angel came to my room last night and told me that I'm going to be alright. I will be in heaven and it will be really nice. I mean it. We don't have to worry anymore at all! And the angel told me that you'll be with me there too someday."

Stu's mouth dropped open. He immediately thought Jada was having delusions from her brain tumor or her medications. He said nothing. But when Jada left the room, he realized that her demeanor had changed, that even her skin looked different. For the first time in months, she looked happy.

Stu and Joaquin, like any parents, were skeptical about what had happened. They shelved it away in the backs of their minds, wishing they could have such reassurance but not willing to believe it.

Jada died about a year after she told her parents about the angel. Never once, however, during the days between her experience and her death did she waver on the truth of her encounter. In fact, she reiterated it often to her parents and said that she—and they—would see each other again and that God, the angel, and heaven were real.

❖ ❖ ❖

The great mystery in life is the existence and activity of the supernatural. Was Jada crazy? If she were the only child who spoke like this, I would say yes. But she isn't. I had another child in a cancer ward tell his crying mother that it was okay for her to go home and sleep at night. "The angel comes," he said, "and helps me and keeps me company while you're gone." I heard this fifteen years before I heard Jada's story.

And there have been others. As a doctor, I believe these testimonies, because the physical descriptions, the feelings, and the resulting peace and confidence are the same.

Doctors witness a lot of pain and sadness. I have come face-to-face with the limitations of men and women. There is only so much that any of us can do for our patients. Our intellect is limited, our knowledge sparse. As Thomas Edison said, "We don't know a millionth of 1 percent about anything."

One advantage that young patients have is that they don't try to rationalize and control everything. They allow human instinct to take over, and when they do, they connect their spiritual dimension to the transcendent.

Your daughter needs a faith in God, because life will inevitably take her to a place where neither you nor anyone else can help. And when she gets there, she will either be alone or put her trust in a loving God. So when she experiences this, do you know what your daughter will do? When neither her own abilities nor your help nor the aid of anyone else will be available, what will she think and what will she feel? Will she pray? Will she know who she's praying to? What she does during those pivotal times in her life depends upon you.

Can you, will you, teach her to turn to God when she needs desperate help?

In a young girl's eyes, you and her mother are the beginning and the end of the line when it comes to love, help, and support. Beyond you, she sees nothing. Many girls who feel emotionally rejected, abandoned, or even simply misunderstood for a period in their lives need to find security somewhere. So they look for something strong, loving, and secure to latch on to. Many turn to God. But others turn to things that are not healthy (drugs, sex, drinking, cults) because they feel so desperate.

Many healthy girls, too, need something other than you to attach to as they mature emotionally and psychologically. This is a normal and healthy process. During her early childhood, your daughter easily attaches to you if you provide enough warmth. As she moves into adolescence, she will begin to pull away from you to see what she can accomplish on her own. But she will still need an anchor while she ventures into new territory. When you're not there as her anchor, she will need something else. Many parents— and teens—will want that something else to be God.

Teens want faith because, I believe, faith in God gives them hope. Your daughter needs hope. We all do. There is so much pain and cynicism in the world that many of us become callous and fatalistic. I hear adults say, "What's the use of anything?" Kids, though, aren't as jaded. They grab on to hope more easily than we do, and we must be sure not to withhold hope from them simply because we're old and crusty.

I was privileged to know a married Jewish couple who survived the Auschwitz concentration camp in World War II. While I met with them only a dozen or so times, they left me with an extraordinary understanding of who God is. When I first met them, I noticed their accents and tattoos. I cringed when I saw the tattoos. I wanted to ask them a million questions. But I was also scared to hear their answers, to learn about the horrors that men can inflict on one another. Reading books had kept me removed. These survivors were flesh and bone.

One evening, they talked about God. They rarely told specific stories of Auschwitz, but they seemed to talk easily about God. At first I was shocked. How could they talk about a good God? How could a good God have allowed such horrific suffering? But I said nothing, and they carried on the conversation with my mother and father, who are Catholic.

"Heda," I heard my mother say, "I have to admit that I don't think that my faith could survive in that situation. How can you really believe that God helped you? If He helped you, why didn't He help everyone else?"

The woman's words were startling. "God didn't make the camp or kill the Jews. The mistake He made was giving men free will and the brains to figure out how to torture people. I knew that He hated Auschwitz more than I did. Many of us had faith. We needed hope. Whether we made it out alive or not, we needed to know that somehow, some way, life would be better. Would it be in heaven? We didn't know what we thought. But God gave me hope and that kept me alive. I couldn't afford wasting energy on hating Him."

Hope kept my friend alive in the concentration camp.

None of us are likely to endure what she did, but all of us will experience pain and loneliness. When that happens to your daughter, she will need faith and hope. Indeed, we know that teens need faith and hope. Suicide is the fourth-highest cause of death among teens.[31] And here's a sobering adjunct: for every adolescent who succeeds in committing suicide, fifty to a hundred others have attempted it.[32] One excellent study revealed that a staggering 33 percent of middle and high school students have thought of killing themselves.[33] The American Psychology Association estimates, based on a variety of studies, that the incidence of clinical depression among teenagers ranges anywhere from between nearly one in ten to nearly one in three (9 percent to 30 percent). All kids who suffer from depression need hope. Terminally ill kids need hope as well. We physicians can often tell the moment a terminally ill patient gives up hope. Death comes very quickly afterward.

One more thing about hope. Girls make a lot of mistakes as they grow up, as we all do. Part of your job as her father is to teach her how to fail well. When she makes a mistake, what then should she do? Should she wallow in self-pity, deny the mistake, or cover it up? None of these are healthy. She needs to be able to recognize a mistake for what it was. If it was a small mistake, help her see it as small. If it was a big one, well, she'll have to face that too.

In order to grow stronger from her mistakes and move forward in an emotionally healthy manner, three things must take place. First, she's got to admit the mistake. Some kids do this a lot better than others. Young kids have a hard time because much of their fantasy lives blends with reality. Be patient if your daughter has difficulty admitting mistakes, but keep at her, because it's a skill she needs to develop.

Second, she must say she's sorry—to you, to whomever she hurt, even to herself. This last gesture is extremely important for teen girls who are sensitive. One of my patients was depressed for eighteen months because she couldn't forgive herself for a big mistake.

Third, she needs to begin her life again, to move forward with a fresh start. Repeatedly I have seen girls, patients of mine, who want to say they're sorry and move forward, but they haven't a clue how to do this; they don't know how to start over. This is what God can offer her: forgiveness, a way to wipe away the past and go back to the starting line. We rarely use the word mercy, but it is a beautiful word. We all know what it means. It is forgiveness and grace when we are down and out. Milton describes God's mercy in *Paradise Lost*: "Through Heav'n and Earth, so shall my glorie excel, / But Mercy first and last shall brightest shine." Forgiveness, mercy, and a fresh start are things every one of us deserves. So, please, give them to your daughter. These will give her hope for her future. If you have a better way to give your daughter hope, go for it. But I don't know any other way. And I have yet to come across anyone who does.

Why You

You are not only the first man in your daughter's life, you are the first authority figure in her life, and your character is invisibly overlaid onto your daughter's image of God. If you are trustworthy, loving, and kind, your daughter will approach God much more easily. He will not be frightening to her. She can understand that He is good, because she knows what goodness in a man looks like.

Research on the influence of a father's personality on his daughter's perception of God confirms this. In one study, researchers found a correlation between children's images of God and those of their father.[34] And girls tend to see more similarities between God and their parents than do boys.[35] A study headed by Hope College professor Jane Dickie found that fathers strongly influenced their daughter's perception of God as nurturing.[36]

In other words, to be a good father is to be a good instructor about God.

❖ ❖ ❖

Heather had a keen interest in knowing God. When I saw her right before she left for college, I asked her how she felt about leaving home.

"Oh, I'm kind of excited but also really sad," she said.

I sensed she wanted to say more, so I asked what she was looking forward to, and what she thought she would miss.

"I'm really excited to live on my own and to live in the city. Also, I think that taking courses that I've never had before will be fun. I'm planning on majoring in Spanish and maybe minoring in political science. See, I want to learn Spanish well enough to go work in an orphanage in another country. You know, some place where kids really need help."

I knew that this poised and confident young woman would do just that. "So how did you get interested in working in an orphanage?" I asked. "Did your folks take you to one? Have you traveled a lot?"

"Oh no, we never traveled much. We didn't have the money. Besides, my dad always worked so much, he never really wanted to take many vacations. He was kind of boring, I guess."

"Then why Spanish and why an orphanage?"

"Now, Dr. Meeker, I know you're gonna think this is kind of crazy and it might not make sense to you, but, well, you see, every morning, my dad and I were the first ones up in our house. I got up after him. Anyway, when I would come downstairs, I always saw him sitting in his chair all alone in the living room. He would be praying. I knew because he had his eyes closed. Or sometimes he would be reading the Bible or a book about the Bible. I knew never to interrupt him.

"My dad has a really strong faith. That's why he got up so early every morning to pray and read the Bible. My dad's a happy man, but he's not one of these guys who talks to everybody. Sometimes he would talk to us about God, but mostly he liked to just live what he learned from his Bible reading in the morning. Anyway, every day I went off to school, I felt so good knowing that my dad had gone to his chair and, I'm sure, prayed for me that day. I can't tell you how good that felt. Somehow, I know that helping poor people, particularly poor kids, would make him really happy. I mean, he wants me to do what I want to, but I really want to be like him. He would do this. And, you know, Dr. Meeker, I want to know what my dad knows about God. I think that working in an orphanage might be a good way to do that. Now I know you think I'm crazy."

"No, Heather, actually I completely get it," I said. Heather didn't tell me that her dad took her to church a lot (although I knew that they did attend a local Methodist church regularly) or that he made her go to Bible study or a youth group. She watched him sit in his chair. That was it. That was all she needed to see to be changed. And he did change her life. He was real and so was his faith. He was quiet, humble, and pursued God. That was all it took to stir something in Heather to want to do the same. Can you begin to see the power you fathers have in your daughters' lives? I'll bet Heather's dad doesn't have a clue how great an impact he's had on her life and faith.

Also, notice that Heather was excited to do something for God because she wasn't afraid of Him. Her dad was genuine and gentle and so, too, she thought, was God. When a daughter has a good relationship with her dad, she very easily and naturally bonds with God. If, on the other hand, you berate her, make sarcastic comments, or are outright cruel to her, she will steer away from God. I have seen over and over again in my practice that girls with good fathers pick good husbands, and girls with good fathers put their trust and faith in God.

What to Do

Whether you believe or disbelieve in God, your daughter will turn to you for answers; and if you believe, she will want to know what He is like. Girls say that their parents are the primary influence over their faith. So get ready.

Before anything else, you have to ask yourself, "What do I believe about God?" Get off the fence. Be courageous and take a stand. If you are unsure, go find out. Read the Bible. Read books directly related to your quest, whether they are popular works like those of C. S. Lewis, straightforward books like Lee Strobel's *The Case for Faith,* or classics like *The Imitation of Christ* by Thomas à Kempis, the *Pensées* of Blaise Pascal, and the novels of Fyodor Dostoevsky. Nothing stretches the limits of human intellect like faith; no other subject has prompted deeper thought than faith in God. So start down the path where the greatest human minds have gone—in a search for God. Start where you are comfortable. Find a good church around you, or take your daughter to temple. Give her something to sink her teeth into and engage her mind. She is hungry for understanding and for knowledge, and if you don't give it to her, I guarantee you that she will find some spiritual information somewhere.

Interestingly enough, kids want religion, but they don't want people to proselytize them.[37] I understand this. I am a New Englander. We leave people alone and keep our business our own. Also, many of the most vocal proselytizers have left a bad taste in our mouths. There is hypocrisy and a sense of manipulation, of something contrived rather than true, and kids rightly reject it.

But your kids trust you and want to hear from you. They know you don't have a secret agenda. They know you to be honest. They know you have their best interests at heart. You have more authority in your daughter's eyes than any pastor, priest, or rabbi. You have an extra load on your shoulders. This is a good thing.

You should know too that kids respect tradition, but without it, and without your guidance, they will fall for fads. For example, the new trend for young people is to believe in something called "Moralistic Therapeutic Deism." The idea is that God exists but that He really isn't involved in anyone's lives; the goal of life is to be happy and feel good about ourselves; and when people die, they all go to heaven.[38]

Kids opt for this "religion lite" because they haven't been given a strong dose of traditional religion from their parents. Kids can't really choose if we withhold religious information from them. It only leaves them ignorant of their Judeo-Christian heritage, which has inspired some of the finest art, music, literature, and philosophy in the world. This is very sad, because across America, our kids are telling us that not only do they want us to teach them about Judaism and Christianity, they want it couched in traditional theology. Research shows that teens like conventional religious traditions and communities.[39] This makes sense. Kids prefer the familiar, and, like most people, they respect and enjoy what has stood the test of time. Traditional religious practice and communities give kids a sense of security and continuity.

They won't get this instruction from the public schools. They won't get it from the mainstream media. And many parents—and even churches—have left kids to fend for themselves. Don't abandon your daughter like this. She wants to know who God is. She wants to know what He is like. And she wants to learn it from you.

St. Augustine said that there is a void in every man's heart that only God can fill. My experience with girls confirms this. Many who aren't given help in understanding God feel restless.

To help your daughter find God, you need to act. I didn't learn about medicine—and you didn't learn about your career—solely through books. I interned in a hospital. I talked to doctors and nurses and patients. When you look for God, go to church or temple. Talk to friends, pastors, rabbis. Get the information you need and make your decision. It might be a decision-in-progress, it might be subject to change, it might take you years to figure out. But get started now, because you need to have answers for your daughter. It is the most important decision you will ever make.

I know these are deeply personal issues that many men would rather avoid, but deep issues shape lives, and they will shape the life of your daughter.

Some grapple with the issue and decide that God really doesn't exist. If you choose atheism, be prepared to defend it to your daughter. She will press you for answers, because most of her friends will believe in God, and she'll want to know why you think differently.

If you believe God exists, don't stop there. Ask yourself: What difference does it make if I do believe in God? When kids were asked whether they felt close to God, the majority of regular churchgoers said yes. Your daughter will want that feeling of relationship with God and will be influenced by how you see your own relationship with Him—if it inspires you to serve others, if it leads you to weekly church or temple attendance, if it encourages you to pray and read the Bible daily, if it grants you a sense of peace and hope, if it gives you strength to deal with calamity. The beauty of fatherhood is that each of you teaches loved ones in your own way, according to your personality.

❖ ❖ ❖

Betsy's father taught her a profound message about God and faith as he was dying. Her father had a rare form of lung disease and he was suffocating. During his life he had been a jovial, hard-working man who took great pride in his work and in providing for Betsy and her siblings. Nearing death, he turned to her and through the whistling of oxygen into his nose he said, "Honey, don't worry about me. I love my Lord and I know He loves me. That's all you ever really need to know. So, I'm fine to go, I'm ready to see Him." Betsy's father gave her peace and a gift to help her overcome her worry and grief.

Be honest, but be willing to move ahead. Don't settle for simply believing that God exists. Your daughter wants more, so give her more. Find out about God. Make it an intellectual journey. Make it a goal to reflect your faith in your behavior: to be more patient, kind, self-controlled, and loving. And remember what science says that faith does for her: highly religious teens do much better in life than less religious teens.[40]

Whether you realize it and want to or not, you will teach your daughter about God and faith. You already are. She will look to you for answers and as a model of faith. Again, research clearly shows that parents are the single most importance influences over daughters' lives when it comes to spiritual and religious issues.[41] And as much as you might shy away from these issues, wouldn't you, as a father, rather have your daughter come to you—and admire your beliefs and how you mirror them—than go to a boyfriend, a neighbor, or some other authority figure? You probably would, and so would your daughter. Don't make it more complicated than it needs to be. If you're not a Bible scholar, pastor, or rabbi, find one and have him or her help you teach your daughter. When you learn to pray, she will. When you change, she will. And when you love God for real, so, too will she. Nothing will bring you closer than this.

Chapter Nine

❖

Teach Her to Fight

My husband is a bona fide eccentric. He hates to travel and loves to spend hours banging around in our woods. When he was a college student at Dartmouth, he made an igloo to sleep in on the weekends (winter only, of course). He competes in any kind of marathon that he can find: biking, cross-country skiing, running, even canoeing. He has finished a few ultra-marathons. He sews exquisitely and has made wool plaid coats for our daughters to keep them warm while they study trees with him. Usually he sleeps about five or six hours a night and often reads Dostoevsky well into the early morning. He doesn't believe in watering our lawn, so every summer our prickly brown grass embarrasses me when friends come over. He drives to work in a beat-up teal pickup with a bumper sticker that says BARF (a type of laundry detergent used in Armenia). And on more than one occasion, he has had patients offer to buy him new shoes.

We share our medical practice, and friends often ask how we manage to be both business partners and marital partners. I find this question perplexing. Surely sharing patients is easier than sharing children. We can disagree about treatments for asthma or pneumonia without any sparks flying. It's a simple difference of professional opinion. But whether we should spank our children? Now there you will find fireworks. Working professionally side by side is really quite easy. His domain is clearly marked, as is mine. But when we come together to sort out what should be done with our children, the issues become muddy. It's not as though our son is his patient and our daughters are mine, or vice versa. They are *our* children—we both have strongly held opinions about how they should be raised, and our desires, beliefs, and emotions are wrapped up in the positions we take. We are both hardheaded and stubborn, and with a joint practice, four kids, and three college tuitions still to pay, you can imagine some of our conversations— especially when I add that my husband and I think about and discuss our child-rearing research and opinions ad nauseum.

After we were married I quickly decided that some of my husband's habits needed changing. For one, he exercised too much. For another, he spent hours at home catching up on work. In both cases, he left me feeling lonely. So I developed a plan.

For the first ten years of our marriage, I studied him (I'm a scientist, after all) and identified what I thought he needed to change. I compiled a hefty unwritten list. Then, over the second ten years of our marriage, I worked to help him make those changes one by one. His "need" to exercise all the time? Nope, I don't think so, not with four kids and a busy household. His workaholic bent? Not in this house. If he had time to listen patiently to all his patients (many of whom were my girlfriends) during office hours, then he certainly had time when he was home to put the phone down, turn off the computer, leave the medical books on the shelves, and talk to me.

I won some battles and I lost some. Finally, for the third decade of our marriage, I've thrown in the towel and decided to leave the man alone. And now I feel embarrassed about all the pushing and prodding I did, because it all seems so selfish. I repeated phrases that you've probably heard countless times yourself, like "I need you with me more"; "I need more help with the kids"; "I want you to communicate better with me." Most women have these thoughts, and they grind away inside us. We want our lives to be easier, and we think "If only he would do this, then my life would be so much better. If only I could get him to understand this, my life would be so much richer."

Fifteen years ago, I scolded my husband for being selfish. That didn't work. Saturdays he had a routine that irritated me. He would walk in from the garage, the metal on the bottom of his bike shoes clattering against the tile on the mudroom floor, and ask, "Do you care if I go on a bike ride?" It was a ridiculous question because his equally brightly clad biking buddies were standing in the driveway waiting for him.

Ten years ago, I pleaded with him to stay home and help me run the kids around. That didn't work. Five years ago, I told him, quietly and lovingly, that he would enjoy his life so much more if he didn't indulge his selfish desires. That didn't work either. Now, when Saturday morning rolls around, I simply say, "Have a good ride." And we're both happier.

When the man wants to ride his bike, he rides his bike. He is who he is, and—guess what?—he's more than enough. He is a good man—a very good man. What I thought I "needed" from him, I had already. What I gave up was my obsession with changing him. My husband knew how to separate the wheat from the chaff. Women can lose sight of that.

Women really are more focused on feelings than men are, and our feelings can become yearnings that leave us constantly desiring more from our husbands. We can wake up thinking, "My day would be so much better if I had a husband who would just pay a little more attention to me."

But husbands have feelings too, which can become equally frustrated. How often have you thought, "I just can't take my wife's obsession with the kids, ignoring me. She acts like they don't even have a father."

Women tend to want more intense relationships. Men tend to want peace and quiet away from work. And both often feel like they are being shortchanged.

Discontentment, frustration, and angst are part of the human experience. But our lives improve when we understand the internal passions that drive us and that drive these emotions. You don't need psychoanalysis or psychotherapy to understand these passions. All you need to do is identify the few internal passions that drive our behaviors and that can dramatically alter the way we live.

Why is this important to you as a father? Because you need to understand that your daughter's emotions are overflowing with impulses that, if acted upon, could lead her toward self-destruction. Your job, as a man, as her father, is to help her keep her emotions in check. It is really quite simple to do, but it takes a tremendous amount of strength and perseverance. And you have to do it, because you will do it better than her mother. Her mother can empathize, but you can guide. You see your daughter more realistically and more objectively than she sees herself. I can't overemphasize how much your daughter needs your direction and authority. From the moment she begins walking, your daughter's emotions, unless they have firm guardrails, can become a threat to her emotional well-being.

Am I exaggerating? You decide as we take a peek into her brain. But there's one thing you can know immediately from your own life. Our passions drive us to do things—or to consider doing things—we know we shouldn't. You have lived with your own intense interior battles. You have learned to deal with your passions, to keep them under control. Sometimes you have gotten it right, sometimes you've really messed up. The point is, you understand internal battles. She doesn't. She feels the tension but has no idea what to do about it. Sometimes she can't even clarify her conflicting emotions and desires.

So first you need to train her to assess her impulses: Are they good or are they bad? Are they encouraging her to be stronger or weaker? Then you must help her identify thoughts, emotions, and desires that should be weeded out, one at a time. Help her to clarify her thinking, help her keep it simple.

And once you do that, teach her to fight. Let her know that you and she are on the same side. Let her know that you will defend her from a very toxic, woman-unfriendly culture.

Train Her Early

Before young children think, they feel. Instincts, which are a form of feelings, cause them to cry when hungry or hurt. You respond because you don't like hearing your baby girl cry. From the moment she is born, your daughter is wired to respond solely on feelings. As she begins to wobble around on her puffy little legs, thoughts start forming, her will kicks into gear, and she starts doing things to evoke responses from you. Watch her body language.

She is one year old and she's walking. She decides to climb the stairs on her own. She knows she shouldn't—you've told her "No!" many times before—but she stretches up the first step. And what does she do after that? She turns around and looks directly at you, waiting for your response. She squats on the second step, thinking, "Should I or shouldn't I?" She's too young to weigh all the pros and cons, but left to herself she will do what she wants. She really wants to go up, so she starts. Her behavior is driven by her wants. What do you do? Well, you either encourage her by walking behind her, or you quickly say "No" and pick her up. You decide. You know what's good for her better than she does.

Well, as much as you might not want to hear this, what's true when she's a toddler is still true when she's sixteen or seventeen. She wants to do what she wants to do (or what others tell her she should do), and she still has not fully developed her ability to think reasonably and abstractly. If you have teenagers, you know teenage logic. They might want to drive really fast down an alley to see what it feels like. They don't imagine crashing into a wall at eighty miles per hour.

From the moment your daughter starts thinking about what she wants to do, you need to challenge her thinking and question her behavior, so that by the time she's a teenager she naturally comes to you to ask, "Dad, this is what I really want to do, but what do you think I should do?" You daughter can know her own feelings, but ultimately, when it comes to making a decision, you know best.

Help your daughter find the balance between feelings, reason, and will. Don't just tell her; show her, in your own behavior, how that balance can be found. Reason, experience, and our moral compass help us decide what to do. As a father, your job is to provide your daughter with a moral compass, to be the voice of reason when she talks about feelings, and to show her the power of will that allows you to live with the outcome of moral reasoning. And you need to accept the fact that many of your daughter's impulses will have to be challenged. Many parents believe, wrongly, that teens have the cognitive skills to be able to "make good choices" on their own. But teenagers are much more driven by feelings than they are by reason. Not only do you need to decide, but you also need to train your daughter from an early age to look to you for decisions. She will never excel at anything if she doesn't learn to respect your help, because you are the one who will determine her ambitions and goals, and you are the one who has to teach her to channel her feelings into useful avenues.

In kindergarten, your daughter might constantly kick another girl's chair, or she might be mouthy to the teacher. Bottom line: When she feels irritated, she kicks. When she wants her own way, she mouths off at the teacher. She is out of control and she *feels* out of control, even though she looks like a tough kid. Even if she was provoked, your daughter needs you to help her separate her feelings from her behaviors. Teach her, over and over again, that she shouldn't always respond to her feelings. Make her practice. If she learns how to do this, she will get along better with others. Just as important, she will feel much more in control of herself.

Some girls are taught by well-meaning parents that their feelings are important, and that they need freedom to "choose their own way." For these girls disaster sits right around the corner. Think about your teenage daughter. Boys call her (on her cell phone of course, so you can't hear the conversation). They send her IMs. The attention feels fun to her. It makes her feel older and more mature. Suddenly she "needs" to go to the movies or roam the mall on Saturday afternoons with a certain fellow. She talks to him on the phone for hours. A couple of his friends "party"—that is, drink or smoke dope—on occasion, but he really is a good kid, she insists. You're a little worried and wonder why she would want to hang out with such a creep. Then you feel guilty about having such thoughts, so you invite him over to the house to check him out. (Note to fathers: always meet your daughters' dates—always.)

He doesn't look too bad, except that his SpongeBob boxers are way above his jeans, which are falling off his butt. "Isn't that uncomfortable?" you wonder silently. But when you see your daughter interact with him, she seems like a different person. She laughs too much and she acts almost aggressive toward him sexually. She touches him and hangs on him. Why? Because when she is with him, her emotions take over and her will evaporates. So watch her like a hawk. Even if you've taught her well, her emotions and "needs" of the moment can still overwhelm her. If you've told her she needs to make her own choices based only on what she "feels," you're in trouble. Worse, she's in trouble.

When she's a little older, college will be a new challenge, and you need to learn about what happens on college campuses these days. Even if you were a partier in college, you'll probably be shocked at the current moral climate on campus. One of my patients is a freshman honors student at the University of Michigan. He told me that during orientation, all freshmen were instructed that they could receive seven condoms *per day* for free. After that they had to pay.

I mention this not to debate the rightness or wrongness of premarital sex, but to tell you that today's colleges cater to sexual appetites that have spun out of control (seven free condoms a day?). It's no surprise that underage drinking is a serious problem on college campuses, but some researchers now compare the level of sexual activity on campus to the sexual activity in brothels.

Brown University recently made the news after a roomful of students (not just five or ten) danced nude or partially nude while drunk. Many had so much to drink that they had to be taken to a local emergency room. Their parents pay $40,000 per year for this.

On campus, the notion of right behavior and wrong behavior—when it comes to sex and alcohol and often drugs—is dead. And where we find desires ruling young men and women, we find self-destruction. The cruelest part is that so many of us adults stand by, shrug our shoulders, and say things like, "Well, kids are kids."

Don't go there. Not with your daughter. Don't put her in situations where her intense, complicated, and passionate feelings will be subjected to so much pressure—and especially don't put her in these situations if you haven't taught her not to give in to her impulses.

Be her ally. Teach her that superficial women feel and respond. You want her to have emotional depth, intellectual wisdom, physical strength, and mental prowess. And none of that can be had without developing her mind and disciplining her will.

Be savvy in choosing your battles. In general, if her food choices, her hairstyle, or her taste in music annoy you, you can let these go (unless they are part of a larger problem—like an eating disorder or hanging out with a bad crowd). Save your energy for the bigger issues that you absolutely need to focus on: honesty, integrity, courage, and humility.

As she grows older her desires will intensify. That's why you need to start early. But it's never too late, especially from her point of view. She wants your guidance, she wants you to talk to her about her decisions—even if she says she doesn't. Left unchallenged, her desires could destroy her. Don't let it happen on your watch.

Clarify Your Morals (without apology)

Until well into her late teens, or even early twenties, your daughter's brain, and her capacity for rational thought, will not be fully developed. The key to communicating with her, aside from listening, is to be very clear about what you say and what you expect. Mixed messages don't stand a chance. Having too many choices overwhelms almost all kids. Of course, they will say just the opposite, but don't believe them. While your daughter might say she wants more choices, she can't handle these choices as well as you can. In fact, too many choices and not enough guidance may make her feel unfocused and powerless.

Give her a set of clear moral guidelines. To do this, you need moral clarity in your mind, and preferably in your life as well. If you don't want her to lie, don't ask her to tell the phone solicitor that you're not home. If you want her to speak respectfully to others and to you, take charge of your tongue. Don't let insults or swear words fly around your house. If you don't want her to get drunk, don't drink too much.

Children are wonderful at forcing us off the moral fence, because they want to know the ground rules for living. They want the facts, they want to know what you think, and they watch what you do.

Don't worry that if you're strict your daughter will rebel or lose her individuality. I have seen over and over again that daughters respect fathers who stand for something. She wants to see conviction and leadership in her father. She might discard your beliefs when she's older, but at least she'll know where you stand. Don't throw her into a wasteland of equivocation by saying, "Well, that depends on how you feel, or how you look at things." Give her something with which to agree or disagree. This teaches her to think, decide, and act.

Your own moral clarity will strengthen her to be her own person one day. A lack of moral clarity on your part may result in your daughter going along with the crowd or assuming that her own unexamined thoughts and feelings are automatically right.

One of the gravest mistakes we parents make is blurring the lines between right and wrong for our daughters. Whatever popular culture does, in your own home with your own daughter, you cannot smudge the lines and rationalize bad behavior. You cannot normalize the bizarre and aberrant; you cannot tolerate rudeness, abuse, or dishonesty. You cannot allow your daughter to risk her future by not confronting her on issues of alcohol, sex, and drugs just because that's the easy thing to do.

When a father suspects his sixteen-year-old daughter is drinking at parties but lets it slide because he can't watch her all the time and "at least she's not driving," if he suspects that his fifteen-year-old daughter is having sex with her boyfriend but doesn't want to talk to her about it and "at least she's not pregnant," if he lets his six-year-old daughter get away with saying "shut up" because "it's funny and harmless," if he defends his seventeen-year-old daughter when she's caught smoking dope because "everybody else was doing it," it might look as if in every case the daughter won. In fact, she lost, because in each case her father let her down. To be a father is to be a leader, to make decisions, to intervene on your daughter's behalf, and to instruct and form her character so that she knows right from wrong, so that she knows when to say no, and so that she's strong enough to fight temptation. And all that requires you to have moral clarity.

Your daughter needs to know your standards, because everyone else is trying to sell her theirs. Here are a few of the most common ones you'll have to battle.

"I Need to Be Beautiful"

I don't have to rage against the marketing of American glamour. You see it, you realize it, you can't escape it. Neither can your daughter. While you pay for your groceries, she peruses fashion magazines. "They're harmless," you console yourself. But you know better. They actually shape the self-assessment of a great many young women. So what can you as a father do?

A lot. Realize that as early as elementary school she is trained to want to look perfect. And while looking good is nice, you—not the glamour magazines—need to set the standards. If you doubt this, I can tell you that I have treated patients with anorexia nervosa who are as young as nine years old.

Many girls begin dieting by the sixth grade. Certainly by junior high they pay close attention to their clothes. Exterior appearance is everything. If she is chubby, she will feel ugly. If she is tall, she will feel geeky. If she is short, she will feel less pretty because all the models are tall.

In high school she will buy whitening strips for her teeth, color her hair (over and over), spend a fortune on haircuts, and may even want plastic surgery. If you live in a large urban area, you are well acquainted with this new craze, for which parents are often to blame. It is now quite common for well-meaning parents to give their daughters plastic surgery as a graduation gift from high school. Frequently these girls opt for breast enlargements before going off to college.

I wish this mistake spoke for itself, but apparently it doesn't. Suffice it to say, it gives your daughter entirely the wrong message, grounds her in superficiality, undermines whatever healthy values she has, and leaves open the question of how much plastic surgery, how much change, is enough to make her beautiful? She should be thinking about excelling in academics, the arts, or athletics, and not about how she can fulfill the X-rated fantasies of young men.

Am I advocating dressing daughters frumpily and turning them into meek wallflowers? Of course not. But trying to be attractive is one thing. Turning wonderful young women into upscale prostitutes is another. And that's what plastic surgery prepares girls for when they go off to the college dorms.

Your daughter's desire to look beautiful is fine if you, as her father, help direct it. The standards should not be MTV's, they should be yours. Don't let her believe that she needs to look one way or another as dictated by popular culture. She is who she is and doesn't need any plastic surgery. She's beautiful just as she is.

❖ ❖ ❖

During her sophomore year at Vanderbilt University, Jackie went home for Christmas break. When her father ushered her into their house he was disturbed by something he saw in her face. Her eyes were darker, grayer, and her eyebrows protruded more than usual. When she took her down coat off, he was shaken. Her breasts were gone and the tiny bones of her shoulders pressed against her cotton shirt. Tom had never seen Jackie look like this. She smiled and he hugged her, carefully. She looked like a baby bird—even her arms and neck were covered with fine hair.

Maybe it was the stress of Vanderbilt that made her look this way, Tom thought. No, he reasoned, it was his divorce. Or maybe it was linked to his bout with depression six years ago—maybe this was something genetic? Or maybe it reflected his shortcomings as a father. Tom worked long hours at his accounting firm and often felt guilty about not being home enough while Jackie and her brothers were growing up.

Over the course of Christmas break, Tom's fears grew. Maybe she had cancer—or AIDS. Possibilities whirled through his mind. He called colleagues, friends, and even his ex-wife. He watched his beautiful daughter get up early every morning and exercise for a full hour and a half in front of a video on the television. He offered to take her out to lunch, then dinner, and she refused both. She was ill-tempered. She said school was going well, but somehow he realized she was lying.

"Why don't you ever eat?" he asked one day.

She screamed at him, "Don't try to control me. You're such a control freak, Dad! Don't you realize I'm an adult now? Mom treats me like one, why can't you? I should have known better than to come to your house for Christmas. Mom warned me."

Tom's heart sank and his thoughts stopped dead. He didn't know what to think or what to do. He called a physician friend. She told him that Jackie probably had an eating disorder.

After Jackie underwent months of intensive medical treatment, I sat beside Tom and his daughter. She was calm and deliberate. He was quiet.

"Dad, you just don't get it. I feel so fat. I know you don't think so, but I know it. The feelings, the thoughts that I'm fat just keep coming back over and over." She sighed heavily.

"Jackie," Tom said firmly. "Tell me that again, please."

"What?"

"Those thoughts—tell me what they say. I want to hear it." He knew what the thoughts were because he'd heard them a million times over. But that wasn't the point.

"Come on, Dad, you know. They say that I'm ugly. If I lost a few pounds then guys would ask me out. Oh, I don't even care about that, I just can't stop feeling like losing a few more pounds would make me feel better."

"Thank you," Tom responded. "That thought's not you. It's the disease talking. Can you push it around? Can you kill it? It's not you, honey. It's those voices in your head that are wrong."

Jackie looked down, frustrated. She didn't argue. In her heart she knew her dad was right. She trusted him. He was smart, he was kind, even if he had made some really big mistakes. He was her dad—and at twenty-two, she listened to him.

"I am beautiful, I am beautiful," he chanted.

Jackie knew what came next. She didn't want to say it. She might believe it. And in some distorted way, starvation had become her friend, and she was afraid to lose it.

Tom waited in silence.

"I am okay-looking," Jackie finally said quietly.

Month after month, Tom's job was to find ways to fight the demons in Jackie's head. He was determined to win.

Jackie returned to Vanderbilt and is doing extremely well today. Did her dad heal her anorexia? Not alone, but his involvement was a necessary part of her treatment.

The best way to prevent anorexia nervosa from striking your daughter is to help her define her self-image, to talk to her often, and if you find she has toxic thoughts, to challenge and defeat them.

"I Need to Be Sexy"

As part of a routine checkup, I leaned over to examine the abdomen of my twelve-year-old patient. She looked up at me and said, "Dr. Meeker, that thing around your neck, it's sexy!"

While I shouldn't have been, I was stunned.

"What thing?"

"You know—whatever that black thing is that you use to listen to my heart. That's so sexy."

Even more disturbing was that the girl's mother didn't flinch as she said these things. She sat in a corner reading her magazine.

Sexy now means cool, pretty, shiny, glamorous, or even just okay. Words can be sexy, book covers can be sexy, even tablecloths can be sexy.

You and I hear the word so often that it becomes devoid of meaning. It's just another word. But we have grown-up minds.

Every day girls see flesh flashed at them by beautiful women: plunging necklines, plump breasts protruding, silky long legs in slit dresses, feet in spiked heels. They see products advertised with sex, they see TV shows relentlessly focused on sex, they listen to music and watch music videos more graphic in sexual imagery than anything experienced by previous generations.

In the mind of a ten-year-old American girl—and certainly if she's older—being sexy is an expected way of life.

Somewhere during her teen years, your daughter will wrestle with the desire to look sexy to her girlfriends and boyfriends. She needs the approval of her peers and longs to live the cool life portrayed in sitcoms and magazines. The voices in her head will tell her that if she isn't sexy, she's nothing.

You don't want your daughter heading off to school with the lace of her red bra peeking out from her unbuttoned white shirt. But our toxic popular culture will tell her that's the thing to do. So you need to teach her otherwise, gently but firmly. Don't make her feel bad about her desire to be attractive. Just affirm that modesty is attractive too—and more self-respecting. Help her to understand what signals she sends to boys through her clothes and behavior. Let her know that you have her best interests in mind; clothing companies don't. She will love you for it.

"I Need to Be Independent"

Strong women are independent. They think on their own, weigh options, and make decisions. Good fathers want their daughters to "stand on their own two feet" and learn to think for themselves.

That's great in theory, but it misses the point that we're all dependent on others—and your daughter is dependent on you.

Many young women have absorbed the feminist idea that women don't need men. Yes, we do. We need fathers, husbands, lovers, protectors, and nurturers. To say that we don't contradicts the most elemental truths of human nature. We need other people. And women need more than just other women.

So while popular culture will teach your daughter she needs to be independent, you need to ensure this is a natural and healthy psychological development (as it can and should be) and not a contrived one. Kids must learn—and earn—their independence.

Where many fathers miss the mark is during adolescence. We've all been trained to believe that teens are "impossible." Adolescence, we're told, is normal and healthy, even if it means your daughter goes through a period of being moody, obnoxious, and out of control. You just have to "give her space."

As a doctor who works with teens, I know that all of that is exactly wrong. "Adolescence" isn't biologically normal. Yes, your daughter will change during puberty, but these changes are physical. The whole image we have of adolescent rebellion and independence does not come from the biochemistry of your daughter; it is—and has been—contrived by modern marketing. It's a "product" you and your daughter don't have to buy.

The idea that parents should leave their teenagers alone only makes it easier to sell this product to your daughter, and actually causes or exacerbates what we think of as "adolescent problems."

Your thirteen-year-old needs you even more than your six-year-old does. Be there for her.

"I Need More"

This one is simple. But it's also widely ignored. Parents simply find it hard to say no when kids say, "But please, Dad, I need..." It starts with toys, then moves up to CDs, televisions in the room, designer-label jeans—you know the score. The problem is not in having things. The problem is thinking that "things" will make you happier. In the old days, parents instinctively understood the danger of spoiling children. Nowadays, parents need to be reminded that giving in to "I need" sets up a vicious cycle of endlessly pursuing material things for the sake of elusive happiness. It leads to greed, anxiety, and meanness.

Does your daughter really need extra toys, bikes, jeans, and shoes in order to make her life better? Of course not. You know that. And she needs to learn it. So act on that knowledge.

"I Can't Say No"

If your daughter is sensitive, sincere, and very nice, you have a serious problem on your hands. Every father alive wants his daughter to display these qualities in addition to being disciplined and wise. These are wonderful aspirations, but you need to be warned.

Nice girls want to please people. Sensitive daughters work very hard to get their fathers' approval. They will go to extremes to receive attention, adoration, and congratulations from you. Be sure that you see this and reassure your daughter that she makes you very happy. But here's the problem. If she is really sweet, she will have difficulty upsetting her friends—she'll find it hard to say no, and they might take advantage of that.

A nice girl needs to be taught to be nice but firm, an[d] and mean it. Teach her to act according to what is bes[t] have her practice saying no, and tell her that the most important part of being nice is living up to the moral code you've given her. Paint scenarios for her so she can visualize what to do. If she goes to a friend's sleepover and the kids are watching *Fatal Attraction*, she needs to leave the room and call you. You know that will be hard for her. She won't want to make a scene, but let her know that the people she has to please most of all are you and her mother, not her friends, who might not know any better, and not her friends' parents, who might have different standards. She needs to politely stand up for her own standards—the ones you've given her.

❖ ❖ ❖

Andrea was eighteen, a senior in high school getting ready to graduate in two months. Her parents left town for the weekend, leaving her to stay home with a girlfriend. Andrea's friend called a boy and invited him over, and pretty soon about thirty kids were at Andrea's home drinking and partying. Andrea felt guilty and frightened and asked people to leave. They wouldn't; they turned the music up louder. One boy was so drunk he fell down the staircase and broke the banister. Another started tossing a medicine ball in the living room and broke a window.

Then the cops came. Most of the kids scattered before the police came to the door. Not Andrea. She stayed, opened the door, and told them everything that had happened. Had she been drinking? "Just a little," she said. A breathalyzer showed she was telling the truth. But she and five of her friends now have police records.

Her school found out. She was kicked off the track team. The college she was entering in the fall found out as well. She started her freshman year on probation.

Her parents shouldn't have left her home alone. Andrea was too nice to be left alone.

❖ ❖ ❖

Parents often tell me, "My daughter is a really good kid. She knows right from wrong and that drinking is trouble. If she were at a party, I have no doubt she would do the right thing."

But I see really good kids all the time who got in trouble because they didn't know how to say no, because their parents hadn't prepared them for the situations in which they found themselves, because their parents expected a teenager to make a decision that an adult should have made. Even the best of daughters want to please their friends. You must assume that whatever her friends do, she'll do.

Finally, remember, nice girls die in car accidents. Nice girls get pregnant. Nice girls fall for bad boys. Teaching your daughter to say no could save her life.

Chapter Ten

❖

Keep Her Connected

"Are you crazy?" I said to my husband. He ignored me. Padding to our children's bedrooms, he whispered, "Come here! I have something to show you." It was 1:30 in the morning.

I stood at the top of the stairs. One by one, he collected our kids and shuttled them outside to the front stoop. There, on the cement, they parked their tired little bodies for the next hour, staring at the northern lights flashing across the sky. Even in June, the night was chilly enough that I could see puffs of air leaving their tiny nostrils. I wanted to scold my husband for putting the kids at risk for pneumonia, but I stayed quiet.

No one said much during that hour in the dark. We simply watched and shivered as brilliant green and red corrugated sheets (they really look like this) streaked through the night. Then we all crept back up the stairs and into our warm beds.

I had difficulty sleeping afterward. The northern lights were beautiful, but what about spelling tests and kids falling asleep in class? I stewed for another half an hour.

I don't remember what grades our children were in that year, let alone what they faced during the next school day. I don't remember because it didn't matter. What matters is that all four of our kids remember their father's extraordinary enthusiasm to share something marvelous with them. They remember sitting in the cold next to their dad—and that it was wonderful.

Psychologists, physicians, and researchers spend untold time and money researching what keeps kids on the right track—away from drugs, gangs, drinking, and sex. And what do they find over and over again? What parents already know: you are the key to your daughter's excellence and happiness.

Parent connectedness: mothers and fathers staying together, and mothers and fathers spending time with their kids. And no one is more important to a daughter than her father.

You don't need to read all the studies and psychology books to know what to do. Our cold little girls connected with their dad on that chilly June night.

All your daughter needs is for you to spend time with her. Think of yourself as your daughter's base camp. She needs a place to stop and settle, to reorient and remember who she is, where she started, and where she's going. She needs a place to rest and get reenergized. You are that place.

Work, Play, and Plan

Fathers like to do things outside the house, so here's a tip: take your daughter with you. Teach her to build an engine. Take her fishing or hiking, or go to a museum, or take her out to dinner. You don't want to turn her into a boy, but let her spend time with you when you're doing what you like to do. It will help you open up and share with her. She'll see you when you are comfortable and enthusiastic. The great thing about outdoor activities is that conversation flows naturally. And especially today, when so many kids live on the Internet and their BlackBerries, having a real flesh-and-blood connection is more important than ever.

Ours is an extraordinarily lonely country filled with people starving for real relationships. Ninety percent of the children (and parents) I see suffering from depression feel deeply lonely. Sophisticated electronics aren't enough. Nothing substitutes for the real live presence of another person.

Experts will tell you that most of what we communicate to another person comes not from what we say, but from our body language. And women are much more sensitive to body language than men are. So when you're with your daughter, focus on her. Don't take her to dinner and constantly glance at the table next to you. She'll notice, and she won't feel the important sense of engagement she otherwise would.

◈ ◈ ◈

Peter and Elizabeth loved athletics and the outdoors. When Elizabeth was in fourth grade, she began running track. When Peter came home from work, he'd take his daughter for a walk in the woods or a jog at the high school track. The more Elizabeth excelled at track, the prouder her father became.

One meet was at a track up on a hill overlooking a four-lane highway. My daughter was competing in the meet as well. At one point, I looked down to the highway, and about half a mile away, I spotted a large gray-haired bicyclist. I finally figured out it was Peter.

He was helmetless and dressed as if he'd come from work, in a white collared shirt with the sleeves rolled up, a tie flapping around his neck, and the legs of his dress slacks pinched into his black socks. Sweat soaked his shirt as he pedaled up the steep hill.

He finally made it to the track, parked his bike, and without combing his tousled hair or even freeing his trousers from his socks headed over to the track.

Elizabeth wasn't running. She was sitting cross-legged on a grassy sideline watching her classmates compete. When she spotted him, she stood up and trotted toward him. He lengthened his stride and quickened his speed. Then he lowered his six-foot-four-inch frame, grabbed her around the waist, and threw her into the air. She squealed as she flew like a rag doll above his head. He caught her, swung her around, and squeezed her. Then she ran back to the track. Her event was up next.

Without any words, Peter connected with Elizabeth. He deepened their relationship. The running didn't make their relationship stronger, spending time together made it stronger. The most vivid connection was when Peter, delighted by Elizabeth's presence, threw her into the air. He didn't ask how she was doing at the meet. He didn't mind looking ridiculous in his bike-riding getup. He immediately and silently communicated that he thought she was wonderful. That was it. That was the connection.

Most mothers don't hoist their fifty-pound fourth graders into the air. We talk to them. Most mothers don't take daughters fishing or help them tinker with engines on the weekends. Fathers do. So do it. Both of you need to get away from chores and homework. You need to spend time together having fun.

The Lonely Teen

Nowadays parents want their children to have cell phones so they can always be in touch. We want them to have e-mail so they can talk to us when they're away at college.

Because music stimulates brain development, we play CDs for kids when they're little and give them iPods when they're older. Then they graduate to BlackBerries.

Most American households now have a computer for every student or worker in the house, because we depend so much on the Internet and word processing. Many girls have televisions in their bedrooms, and older girls have not only televisions but laptops, cell phones, and sound systems as well. Girls' bedrooms have become cozy electronic havens enticing them to play, relax, or "connect" with their friends for hours at a time.

Kids spend more time immersed with electronics than ever before. This is the way life is. But it carries some very serious psychological risks. Even though girls think they're using electronics to connect, when they use a computer, a cell phone, or an iPod, they're really alone. They're not face-to-face with anyone. While electronic relationships are real, they are profoundly limited and even dangerous.

Consider your daughter's cell phone. If she is a normal fourteen-year-old, the moment she leaves school, she hops on a bus and dials her friend. They chat about peculiar and often nonsensical matters. Instead of seeing her friend, her mind retrieves images of her that might accompany her speech. If her girlfriend laughs, she conjures up that image; if they argue, she imagines the scowl in her friend's eyes. She feels as though they are together, but they aren't.

Then she goes home and starts instant messaging. A few more girlfriends jump online and they chat. She speaks, but no one hears her voice. There are no verbal inflections, and it's nearly impossible for her to visualize her friends. She is communicating, but only through misspelled words and mystifying abbreviations. Words, of course, are very powerful. They can stir emotion and they can accompany emotion, but only if they are communicated well—and communicating well doesn't happen with teenagers using IM.

Now she logs off and bounds to her bedroom to relax or do homework. She puts on her headphones to listen to her iPod.

Music filters into her ears. She no longer communicates with anyone at all.

After dinner, she logs on to her e-mail. She sends messages that disappear and then reappear on someone else's screen. She is communicating but, again, alone.

If your daughter is an average girl, she will spend between six and eight hours a day with electronic tools of some sort. Parents often don't mind, because if their children are playing with electronics, it frees mom and dad and allows them to spend time away from the kids and finish paying bills, make phone calls, or even just read the newspaper. So while electronics might help you get things done, they also dramatically decrease the time you spend with your children. That alone hurts your relationship with your daughter.

In the meantime, your daughter is making connections that aren't real flesh-and-blood relationships. E-mail is less real than IM, and IM is less real than cell phones, and cell phones are less real than talking face-to-face.

The majority of American girls love instant messaging. Girls not only speak more words than boys, they type more. In IM, words can be dressed up with question marks, exclamation points, and smiley faces. IM language can be cute, entertaining, and fun for kids to use, but it's also far removed from real human contact. You might find that after a while your daughter will have difficulty talking with you in a car, room, or restaurant, because being face-to-face is powerful and frightening, and she's too used to the anonymity of electronics. When she sees your face, there is no escaping your feelings or your thoughts. Real life becomes over-stimulating to her senses. Voices are loud. Touch is foreign. Eyes pierce and crush her hopes. You are a distant and frightening figure.

Don't let this happen. There's no need to banish electronics, but make sure that time online is balanced with time with you. Phone calls aren't good enough. You need to be together. This is critical to her healthy emotional, intellectual, and physical development. You need to recognize that your daughter is being trained to relate very differently from the way you were taught. It's a cliché that men have greater difficulty with intimacy than women. I'm not so sure that's true any longer—at least not with fathers and daughters. You spend hours in face-to-face conversations; she spends hours in chat rooms. You can recognize what's real. She can't always see it.

Since you are competing with e-conversations, e-songs, and e-relationships, steal her away from the screen as often as you can. Remember, when all is said and experienced, you are a better communicator than cell phones, e-mail, or chat rooms. They can't comfort her when she's in the hospital. They can't walk her down the aisle toward her future husband. You will.

Aside from stealing time away from you, e-communications pose another danger to your daughter. They encourage a lack of truthfulness. IM has taken on a life of its own because of this phenomenon. Specifically, kids lie with regularity in a way they wouldn't do face-to-face. They don't do it because they're bad kids, but because it's fun. They use a lot of foul language for the same reason. So girls say things to boys over IM that they would never say to them in person. Some have "cyber-sex" with one or more friends, even friends in their class they've only spoken a few words to. Computer screens loose inhibitions.

Most girls hate bad language, but they embrace it on IM because bad language, half-truths, outright lies, pretending to be another person, and verbal pornography are all part of the IM world, which, to young girls, seems fun and harmless. But you know better, and you know that what starts on a computer screen can end in trouble.

So keep her grounded in reality, be truthful with her, expect truthfulness from her, and don't let computers come between you.

Surviving Stress

No one likes to seek out stressful situations, but surviving stressful times together creates powerful bonds. If there is stress in your life—and whose life doesn't have stress?—use it to bond with your daughter by bringing her with you. A problem to solve, a project to complete together (even simple things, like pitching a tent while camping or tinkering with a broken engine) can be great. Watch what happened between Elliott and Hillary.

❖❖❖

When Elliott was seventy years old, he retired from his thriving practice of general surgery. He didn't like retirement. He was neither a golfer nor a fisherman. He didn't like tinkering around the house. So, in his boredom, at age seventy, he asked his forty-six-year-old daughter Hillary, also a physician, to accompany him on a two-week medical trip to Nicaragua. She agreed.

When the two of them arrived in Nicaragua, Elliott was beaming. Hillary was nervous about dirty toilets, undrinkable water, and annoying bugs, but Elliott was oblivious to them. She worried about how he would deal with the heat, how he might get sick with a tropical disease, or how he might break an arm or a leg and have to be evacuated—somehow—to the United States. But Elliott didn't worry at all.

After a few days of collecting supplies and traveling deep into the countryside, they and their team set up a clinic where they could evaluate patients. If any needed surgery, they'd drive them to the nearest hospital and perform the operation.

One woman had a tumor the size of a grapefruit in her uterus. Two young men had inguinal hernias; another had a testicular mass. Elliott loved using his broken Spanish and diagnosing his patients. He was exhilarated.

That was before he saw the "hospital." Hillary and a nurse well versed in anesthesia accompanied him. As they drove up the dirt road to the hospital, Elliott gasped. The building was abandoned. There was no electricity, though at least there was running water. The bus driver politely ushered him through a doorless entryway into an eight-by-eleven-foot room with a single window. A steel operating table sat in the middle of the room. A large lamp hovered above it. It had no bulb and its glass casing was shattered. Elliott began sweating.

In the doorway, the first patient—a young man with a hernia—waited.

Hillary saw her father's ashen face. She took a deep breath and said, "Come on, Dad, you can do this. Hernias are easy. That's what you've always told me. We can get this done." She gestured to the nurse, who began setting up her station of medicines and portable oxygen.

"It's filthy. What about infection? This poor guy will die of an infection."

"No, Dad. We'll take it one step at a time. I've got IV meds, IV fluid, and some pain meds. I'll take care of all that. You just operate."

Hillary motioned to the young boy to wait a few more minutes while they got everything prepared. She wiped the table and pulled the sterile instruments, gowns, and drapes from her trunk. She felt herself trembling. The room was hot and humid.

But they proceeded. Elliott repaired his first patient's hernia. Then he fixed another. Then he removed the woman's tumor and the man's testicular mass. Every few minutes he wiped his sweating brow on his sleeve. It broke sterile code, but he had no choice. He had to see. There was no air conditioning, and several times Elliott thought he would pass out. Hillary watched him and watched his patients. After three days of surgery and twelve patients—half of whom developed infections or had uncontrollable pain—Elliott had had enough.

He sat with the rest of the team at dinner, choking down canned green beans and warm potatoes. Clean water was running low.

"I'm done," he announced. "I'm sorry. I just can't do this anymore. I can't operate well. My patients are getting infections and I'm doing them more harm than good."

Elliott was a Texan, six-feet-two. He began to cry.

But the team told him not to quit. Hillary in particular encouraged her father, saying that although she wasn't a surgeon, she knew enough about surgery to assist him, especially when he felt tired and needed to sit down.

So Elliott, operating side by side with his daughter, finished the two-week medical trip. By the end, he was emotionally and physically exhausted. On the plane back to the United States he was too tired to talk.

Hillary will tell you now, since her father's death, that that trip made their relationship extraordinarily close. As a kid, she had given her parents trouble. But she knew her father was a good man, a very good man, and, especially after their work together in Nicaragua, she felt privileged to have lived her life with him. She had seen him stretching himself to the utmost to help others. She had helped him—and he had wanted her there at his side. "He knew me and he loved me. What more could I ask for in a dad?"

❖ ❖ ❖

Can you connect with your daughter? Absolutely. Keep it simple. Make it part of your everyday life. Have her help you with chores, or take her out to the theater, or go on a mission trip with her, but whatever you do, focus on her. Tune in to her, listen to her, and don't let work and its preoccupations distract you from your daughter. At the end of the day, she's more important than anything else.

Afterword

Every day is a challenge. The daily grind of work is tough. And what keeps us going is the hope that at the end of the day, life will be a little better, happier, calmer, and more joyful, that our anxiety might cease, that our internal ache for "something more" might be assuaged.

Many days we are disappointed. We find ourselves grasping for that elusive "something" that will make us feel more complete. But the more we search for it, the more distant it becomes, because what we're searching for is sitting right there. It's not your job or your hobbies. It's not more money or more sex. It's your family— your children, your spouse—and God. They are the real center of our lives. Men who figure this out find what they're looking for. Men who don't are never truly happy and satisfied.

The problem is that it's very easy for us to lose perspective. There are a million distractions and temptations. They pull at us and can lead us astray.

We adults are not alone in this; our children, too, are easily led astray. Every day, your daughter faces similar temptations. Every day, she will need your guidance and example to understand why life is a great gift and how she should use it.

Reading this book would not be worth the time it took unless you put its ideas into action. So here are some final tips to guide your action plan.

Realize Who You Are to Her

When she is a baby, her eyes will search for your face. Her ears will listen for your voice and everything inside her will need to answer only one question, "Daddy, are you here?" If you are there, her body will grow better. Her IQ will start to rise, her development will track where it is supposed to, but more important, she will realize that life is good because you love her. You are her introduction to love; you are love itself.

When she goes to kindergarten she will think about you and she might even talk about you. If another classmate makes a hurtful remark, your daughter will boast to the bully that he'd better be careful because you, her hero, will come over to his house and beat him up. To her, you can do anything, and, most especially, you can protect her.

In elementary school, her challenges and her world expand, but her question for you will be the same: "Daddy, are you still there for me?" When she is thirteen and wearing lipstick, or fifteen and competing in a spelling contest, or seventeen and living at a friend's house because she can't stand you, one question alone will haunt her: "Dad, are you there for me?" She needs to know that the answer is always yes. The more you leave her wondering, the harder she will push for an answer—and she might go to extremes to try to force it from you.

And when she has her first child, or is diagnosed with breast cancer at thirty, or her husband walks out on her and her kids, the question will remain: "Dad, please, Dad, are you there?"

If she knows that you are there, dependable and full of love for her, you will have taught her this great lesson: Life is good. Good men help make it so.

Open Your Eyes to Her World
(it's different from yours)

Being a father isn't easy. You will face a series of roadblocks, and most of them will come from the culture into which she's born, rather than from anything you've done.

First and foremost, school will pull her away from you. Is school a bad thing? Of course not, but some of her experiences at school can work against your relationship with her. She will hear things you don't want her to hear. She will hear derogatory remarks about things you believe. She might even hear criticism of you. She will be taught sex education, which can harm her, and when that happens, she might feel embarrassed and hide from you. Her friends and peers might try to pull her away from you. This is life in the twenty-first century: what's a dad to do?

A lot. A whole lot. You might not be able to single-handedly change popular culture or reform school curricula, but what you say and do, the example you set, and the leadership you provide can absolutely keep your daughter on the right track—or put her back on it. Your influence is that important. And even if you feel that it's too late, that she's too far gone from you, run to find her. It doesn't matter how old you are or how old she is. She is still your daughter. You are still her father.

Fight for Her Body

By far the greatest danger to your daughter comes from the aggressive marketing of sexuality that, unchecked, can give her a horribly skewed sense of self. In elementary school she will be encouraged to be sexy, to watch sex on television or DVDs. Music, clothing, toys, video games, and magazines she spies while shop-ping will be soaked with sex. Why are these images and messages so devastating? Because from the time she is seven, sex (whatever that means to her) will be on her young mind. And if she starts having sex during her teen years, she puts herself at tremendous health risk. Truthfully, I would prefer that my teen patients (and my own kids) smoke during their teen years rather than have sex. Think about it. If a sixteen-year-old girl smokes until she's twenty and then stops, her lungs and her cardiovascular system will recover and she can be completely healthy for the rest of her life. If she is sexually active during these same years, on the other hand, she stands a reasonable chance of contracting a sexually transmit-ted disease. Some she may recover from. Others she may not. Once she contracts herpes—either type 1 or type 2—she's got it for life. Or she may become repeatedly infected with HPV and develop cer-vical cancer. And then there's the real possibility of fertility prob-lems caused by an infection in her reproductive organs. Many sexually transmitted infections do not show any symptoms until it's too late.

Don't let this happen to your daughter, please. Protect her mind, protect her body. Remember, setting rules has nothing to do with trust—particularly during the teen years. Setting rules and being vigilant about protecting her is a matter of her anatomy and emo-tions, and your parental responsibility. Her brain is not fully devel-oped. Scientists now know so much more about the teen brain than we did a decade ago, and what we've learned makes parental authority crucial. We know that regardless of a girl's personality, intelligence, or grade point average, she does not have the intel-lectual maturity of an adult, and she can be easily seduced into trouble. But you can keep her out of it. So meet her boyfriends. Don't let her wander alone at night with them. Err on the side of being overprotective and you'll hit it just right, because even if you feel more unreasonable than her friends' parents, remember, they've got the problem of being too naïve. Compared to them, you might appear strict, but you'll be less likely to have problems with your children in the future. Protect her and defend her, and your daughter will know that you love her.

Fight for Her Mind

She will diet, think about carbs and breasts, small waists and emaciated arms. She will wonder whether muscle is good or bad. You won't, but she will. She might even be obsessive in thinking about her body. These thoughts endanger her sense of self-worth. You need to be aware that they're in her head, and you need to help her fight them. You need to teach her that she is valuable because she is human, that she is beautiful as she is, that much of what she sees on TV, in the movies, and in magazines is a lie and an illusion. Engage your daughter in this conversation and you'll be amazed how well it works and how much it will enhance your relationship with her. You are a warrior in her eyes. You of all people know how to fight, because you are her dad—so get into the battle and help her.

Never let popular culture steal your daughter from you. Teach her the centrality of family, the importance of humility, and the rewards of helping others. Teach her to look beyond herself.

Fight for Her Soul

And then there's faith. Your daughter will wonder and ask about death and the supernatural. She will want to ask questions. Something inside her will prompt her to know if God is real, and if He is, what He's like. So help her. Don't back out. Just as you teach her to ride a bike, to know right from wrong, to stay away from drugs, teach her about God. She is a spiritual being and she wants answers to her questions. More than that, it is a simple fact that faith is good for her. This is demonstrable in study after study. So dive in. Get her to church or temple, teach her to pray, open the Old Testament and the New and see what's there. Understanding God is the most important intellectual and spiritual journey anyone makes. Don't leave her out of it.

Fight for Your Relationship with Her

What your daughter wants most from you is your time. Don't be anxious about spending time with her. Many fathers think they need to entertain their daughters to make the time seem special. This is particularly true of divorced fathers. But your daughter doesn't need—or even want—special events or outings. She just needs to be with you, next to you doing chores, washing the car, living life. So just live it with her. Ask her to rake leaves with you, go grocery shopping, or change the oil. And let her know that you need her help. If she is fifteen and wants to go to the mall on a Saturday afternoon, either go with her and make it an outing, or don't let her go. Instead, make her stay home and help you around the house. The bottom line is: she needs more time with you than she does with her friends. So be with her.

Your daughter looks to you for guidance, whether the issue is what instrument or sport to play, what college to attend, or what to do about sex, drinking, and drugs. If she feels close to you, she's much more likely to make good decisions. If she doesn't feel close to you, all bets are off.

So keep her connected: talk to her, spend time with her, and enjoy your time with her, because she is growing every day. You can bring extraordinary richness to your daughter's life and she can bring immeasurable rewards to yours.

One day, when she is grown, something between the two of you will shift. If you have done your job well, she will choose another good man to love her, fight for her, and be intimately connected to her. But he will never replace you in her heart, because you were there first. And that's the ultimate reward for being a good dad.

Acknowledgments

I would like to extend many thanks to the wonderful people who helped me make this book great. First, I would like to thank Doug and Judy for the extraordinary way you live your lives. Your inspiration is infectious and your faith exemplary.

I would like to also thank the wonderful folks at Regnery, who published the original manuscript in hardcover. Thank you, Marji Ross, for your encouragement and example of how a strong woman lives. To Karen Anderson, thank you for your enthusiasm and wit, and for helping launch my writing career. To my editor, Harry Crocker, thank you for being so wise, patient, and such a good man. To Paula Currall and Kate Morse, thank you for your expertise in final editing. To Angela Phelps, thank you for your enthusiasm and thoroughness. And thanks to my terrific research assistant, Jill Pardini.

Finally, I thank my great friend Anne Mann for your dedication, amazing patience, and love.

Bibliography

Adler, Mortimer J., ed. *The Great Ideas: A Syntopicon of Great Books of the Western World, Vol. II.* New York: Encyclopedia Britannica, Inc., 1971.

Allen, David, M.D. *Shattering the Gods Within.* Chicago: Moody Press, 1994.

Bengtson, Vern L. "Beyond the Nuclear Family: The Increasing Importance of Multi-Generational Bonds." *Journal of Marriage and Family* 63 (February 2001): 1.

Blackman, Maurice. "Adolescent Depression." Originally published in *Canadian Journal of CME*, May 1995. http://www.mentalhealth.com\mag1\p51-dp01.html.

Bradley, Robert H., et al. "The Home Environments of Children in the United States Part 2: Relations with Behavioral Development through Age 13." *Child Development* 72 (November 2001).

Cavanagh, C. Kate. "The Father-Daughter Relationship." *Annals of the American Psychotherapy Association* 5 (May–June 2002): 28 (1).

Centers for Disease Control and Prevention. National Center for HIV, STD, and TB Prevention, to Visions of HIV/AIDS Prevention. "Young People at Risk: HIV/AIDS Among America's Youth." http://www.cdc.gov\hiv\pubs\facts\youth.htm

Collins, Stuart, et al. "High Incidence of Cervical Human Papillomavirus Infection in Women During Their First Sexual Relationship." *British Journal of Obstetrics and Gynecology* 109 (2002): 96–98.

Cox, Melissa R., ed. *Questions Kids Ask About Sex: Honest Answers for Every Age.* Grand Rapids, MI: Revell, 2005.

Crabb, Larry. *Connecting Healing for Ourselves and Our Relationships.* Nashville: W Publishing Group, 1997.

Culp, A. M., M. M. Clyman, and R. E. Culp. "Adolescent Depressed Mood, Reports of Suicide Attempts, and Asking for Help." *Adolescence* 30 (1995): 827–37.

Deater-Deckard, Kirby, David W. Fulker, and Robert Plomin. "A Genetic Study of the Family Environment in the Transition into Early Adolescence." *Journal of Child Psychology and Psychiatry* 40 (July 1999): 769.

DeLamater, John, and William N. Friedrich. "Human Sexual Development." *Journal of Sex Research* 39(1) (February 2002): 10(5).

Dickie, Jane R., et al. "Parent-Child Relationships and Children's Images of God." *Journal for the Scientific Study of Religion* 36 (March 1997): 25–43.

Dickinson, Amy. "Dads and Daughters: Strengthening This Special Relationship Can Strengthen a Girl's Self-Esteem Too." *Time* (May 13, 2002).

Doherty, William J., Ph.D., Edward F. Kouneski, M.A., and Martha Farrell Erickson, Ph.D. "Responsible Fathering: An Overview and Conceptual Framework." University of Minnesota (September 1996).

Eng, Thomas R., and William T. Butler, eds., Committee on Prevention and Control of Sexually Transmitted Diseases, Institute of Medicine. *The Hidden Epidemic*. Washington, DC: National Academy Press, 1997.

Fabes, Richard A., et al. "Parental Coping with Children's Negative Emotions: Relations with Children's Emotional and Social Responding." *Child Development* 72 (May–June 2001): 907.

"Facts in Brief: Teen Sex and Pregnancy." 1995 National Survey of Family Growth and 1995 National Survey of Adolescent Males. New York: The Alan Guttmacher Institute, 1998.

Fleming, D. T., et al. "Herpes Simplex Virus Type 2 in the United States 1976 to 1994." *New England Journal of Medicine* 337 (1997): 1105–60.

Fortenberry, J. Dennis. "Unveiling the Hidden Epidemic of Sexually Transmitted Diseases." *Journal of the American Medical Association* 287 (2002): 768–69.

Graydon, John. "Depression." University of Michigan Advances in Psychiatry Audiology Library 30, no. 16 (2002).

Greenlee, Robert, Taylor Murray, Sherry Bolden, and Phyllis A. Wingo. "Cancer Statistics 2000." *CA: A Cancer Journal for Clinicians* 50 (2000): 7–33.

Guidelines for Comprehensive Sexuality Education, Kindergarten–12th Grade, second edition. National Guidelines Task Force. New York: Sexuality Information and Education Counsel of the United States, 1996.

Gutzwiller, Joeanne, Ph.D., J. M. Oliver, Ph.D., and Barry M. Katz, Ph.D. "Eating Dysfunctions in College Women: The Roles of Depression and Attachment to Fathers." *Journal of American College Health* 52, no. 1: 27–32.

Hallfors, Denise D., Ph.D., et al. "Which Comes First in Adolescence: Sex and Drugs or Depression?" *American Journal of Preventive Medicine* 29 (2005): 163–70.

Hertel, Bradley R., and Michael J. Donahue. "Parental Influences on God Images Among Children: Testing Durkheim's Metaphoric Parallelism." *Journal for the Scientific Study of Religion* 34 (June, 1995): 186–99.

Horn, Wade F., Ph.D., and Tom Sylvester. *Father Facts,* fourth edition. Gaithersburg, MD: National Fatherhood Initiative, 2002.

————. *Father Facts* research notes. National Fatherhood Initiative, http://www.fatherhood.org.\fatherfacts_rsh.asp.

Huston, Aleatha C., Ellen Wartella, and Edward Donnerstein. *Measuring the Effect of Sexual Content in the Media.* Menlo Park, CA: The Henry J. Kaiser Family Foundation, May 1998.

Jones Jessop, Dorothy. "Family Relationships as Viewed by Parents and Adolescents: A Specification." *Journal of Marriage and the Family* 43 (February 1981): 95–107.

Kelly, Joe. "Dads and Daughters: Grassroots Advocacy." *Pediatric Nursing* 27 (July 2001): 391.

à Kempis, Thomas. *The Imitation of Christ.* New York: Dorset Press, 1952.

Kenny, Maureen E., and Laura A. Gallagher. "Instrumental and Social\Relational Correlates of Perceived Maternal and Paternal Attachment in Adolescence." *Journal of Adolescence* 25 (2002): 203–19.

Knafo, Ariel, and Shalom H. Schwartz. "Parenting and Adolescents' Accuracy and Perceiving Parental Values." *Child Development* 74 (March 2003): 595.

Knox, Sarah S., Ph.D., et al. "Measuring Parenting from an Epidemologic Perspective." National Children's Study Workshop, October 4, 2004. http://www.nationalchildrensstudy.gov\events\workshops\measuring_parenting_102004.cfm.

Kunkel, Dale, et al. "Sex on TV: Content and Context." Menlo Park, CA: The Henry J. Kaiser Family Foundation, 1999.

Larson, David B., M.D., M.S.P.H., and Susan S. Larson, M.A.T. "The Forgotten Factor in Physical and Mental Health: What Does the Research Show? An Independent Study Seminar." Rockville, MD: National Institute for Health Care Research, 1994.

Levine, Michael, Ph.D. "10 Things Parents Can Do to Help Prevent Eating Disorders." National Eating Disorders Association, 2005. http://www.nationaleatingdisorders.org.

Lickona, T., and M. Davidson. *Smart & Good High Schools: Integrating Excellence and Ethics for Success in School, Work, and Beyond*. Cortland, NY: Center for the 4th and 5th Rs (Respect and Responsibility); Washington, DC: Character Education Partnership, 2005.

Lynn, David B. "The Husband-Father Role in the Family." *Marriage and Family Living* 23 (August 1961): 295–96.

Mansfield, Harvey. *Manliness*. New Haven and London: Yale University Press, 2006.

————. "The Manliness of Men." *American Enterprise* 14 (2003): 32–34.

McGuire, Shirley, et al. "Perceived Competence and Self-Worth During Adolescence: A Longitudinal Behavioral Genetic Study." *Child Development* 70 (November–December 1999): 1283–96.

Moore, Mignon R., and P. Lindsay Chase-Lansdale. "Sexual Intercourse and Pregnancy among African American Girls in High-Poverty Neighborhoods: The Role of Family and Perceived Community Environment." *Journal of Marriage and Family* 63 (November 2001): 1146.

Morbidity and Mortality Weekly Report Surveillance Summaries, Vol. 53 (May 21, 2004): 1–20. http://www.cdc.gov/mmwr/.

Mueller, Walt. *Understanding Today's Youth Culture*. Wheaton, IL: Tyndale House Publishers, Inc., 1994.

National Center for HIV, STD, and TB Prevention, Centers for Disease Control, U.S. Department of Health and Human Services. "Tracking the Hidden Epidemics." http://www.cdc.gov.

National Institute of Allergy and Infectious Diseases, National Institutes of Health, Department of Health and Human Services. "Workshop Summary: Scientific Evidence on Condom Effectiveness for Sexually Transmitted Disease Prevention," July 20, 2001.

"New Study Finds Kids Spend Equivalent of Full Work Week Using Media." Press Release, The Henry J. Kaiser Family Foundation, November 29, 1999.

Nicholi, Armand M. Jr., ed. *The Harvard Guide to Psychiatry*, third edition. Cambridge, MA: The Belknap Press of Harvard University Press, 1999.

O'Malley, William J., S.J. *God: The Oldest Question*. Chicago, IL: Loyola Press, 2000.

Parmelee, Dean X. *Child and Adolescent Psychiatry*. St. Louis, MO: Mosby Publishing, 1996.

Pascal, Blaise. *The Provincial Letters; Pensees; Scientific Treatises*. Chicago, IL: Encyclopedia Britannica, Inc., 1971.

Smith, Christian, and Melinda Lundquist Denton. *Soul Searching: The Religious and Spiritual Lives of American Teenagers*. New York: Oxford University Press, 2005.

Strobel, Lee. *The Case for Faith: A Journalist Investigates the Toughest Objections to Christianity*. Grand Rapids, MI: Zondorvan, 2000.

"The National Longitudinal Study of Adolescence," 1997: 1–35. http://www.cpc.unc.edu\addhealth.

Tozer, A. W. *The Pursuit of God: The Human Thirst for the Divine*. Camp Hill, PA: Christian Publications, Inc., 1982.

Volkmar, Susan. "Child-Father Interaction May Predict Suicide Reattempts." *Clinical Psychiatry News* 33 (August 2005): 63.

Walboomers, J. M., et al. "Human Papillomavirus Is a Necessary Cause of Invasive Cervical Cancer Worldwide." *Journal of Pathology* 189 (1999): 12–19.

Wald, A., A. G. M. Langenberg, K. Link, et al. "Effect of Condoms on Reducing the Transmission of Herpes Simplex Virus Type 2 from Men to Women." *Journal of the American Medical Association* 285 (2001): 3100–06.

Wenk, Dee Ann, et al. "The Influence of Parental Involvement on the Well-being of Sons and Daughters." *Journal of Marriage and Family* 56 (February 1994): 229–34.

Yancey, Philip. *Soul Survivor: How 13 Unlikely Mentors Helped My Faith Survive the Church*. New York: Galilee and Doubleday, 2001.

Yeung, W. Jean, et al. "Children's Time with Fathers in Intact Families." *Journal of Marriage and Family* 63 (February 2001): 136.

Zhou, Qing, et al. "Personality and Social Development: The Relations of Parental Warmth and Positive Expressiveness to Children's Empathy-Related Responding and Social Functioning: A Longitudinal Study." *Child Development* 73 (May–June 2002): 893.

Notes

Chapter One: You Are the Most Important Man in Her Life

1. "Guidelines for comprehensive sexuality education," The Sexuality Information and Education Council of the United States, 2004, found at: http://www.siecus.org/pubs/guidelines/guidelines.pdf, 51–66.
2. "Sex on TV," Kaiser Family Foundation, (2005) found at: http://www.kaiserfamilyfoundation.org/entmedia/upload/sex-on-TV-4-Executive-Summary.pdf.
3. Ibid.
4. D. T. Fleming et al., "Herpes Virus Type 2 in the United States, 1976 to 1994," *New England Journal of Medicine* 337 (1997): 1105–60.
5. Ibid., 5.
6. Surveillance Summary, *Morbidity Mortality Weekly Review* 53 (May 21, 2004).
7. Margaret J. Blythe et al., "Incidence and Correlates of Unwanted Sex in Relationships of Middle & Late Adolescent Women," *Archives of Pediatric & Adolescent Medicine* 160 (2006): 591–95.
8. Meg Meeker, *Epidemic: How Teen Sex Is Killing Our Kids* (Washington, DC: LifeLine Press, 2002), 154–55.

9. Ibid.
10. Surveillance Summary, *Morbidity Mortality Weekly Review* 53: 17.
11. American Social Health Association, *Sexually Transmitted Diseases in America: How Many Cases and at What Cost?* (Menlo Park, CA: Kaiser Family Foundation, 1998).
12. J. M. Walboomers et al., "Human Papillomavirus Is a Necessary Cause of Invasive Cervical Cancer Worldwide," *Journal of Pathology* 189 (1999): 12–19.
13. Bosch et al., "Effect of oral contraceptives on risk of cervical cancer in women with the human papillomavirus infection: the IARC multicentric case-control study," International Agency of Research on Cancer.
14. Fleming et al., "Herpes Virus Type 2 in the United States, 1976 to 1994."
15. http://medinstitute.org/includes/downloads/herpes.pdf.
16. Surveillance Summary, *Morbidity Mortality Weekly Review* 53: 8–16.
17. Denise Halfors, "Which Comes First in Adolescence: Sex and Drugs or Depression?" *American Journal of Preventive Medicine* 29 (2005): 3.
18. Surveillance Summary, *Morbidity Mortality Weekly Review* 53: 9.
19. Ibid., 16.
20. Ibid., 12.
21. Ibid.
22. Ibid.
23. Ibid.
24. Ibid.
25. "Generation M: Media in the Lives of 8–18 Year-Olds," Kaiser Family Foundation, March 2005. See: http://www.kaiserfamily-foundation.org/entmedia/upload/Executive-Summary-Generation-M-Media-in-the-lives-of-8-18-Year-olds.pdf.
26. Ibid., 23
27. Ibid., 12.
28. Ibid., 25.
29. Ibid.
30. Ibid.
31. Ibid.

32. M. Esterbrooks and Wendy A. Goldberg, "Toddler Development in the Family: Impact of Father Involvement and Parenting Characteristics," *Child Development* 55 (1984): 740–52.

33. F. A. Pedersen et al., "Parent-Infant and Husband-Wife Interactions Observed at Five Months," in *The Father-Infant Relationship* (New York: ed. F. Pedersen, 1980), 65–91.

34. Ibid.; Rebekah Levine Coley, "Children's Socialization Experiences and Functioning in Single-Mother Households: The Importance of Fathers and Other Men," *Child Development* 69 (February 1998): 219–30.

35. Coley, "Children's Socialization Experiences and Functioning in Single-Mother Households."

36. A. Morcoen and K. Verschuren, "Representation of self and socioemotional competence in kindergartners: differential and combined effects of attachment to mother and father," *Child Development* 70 (1999): 183–201.

37. *Journal of the American Medical Association* 10 (September 10, 1997): 823–32.

38. Ibid.

39. *American Journal of Preventive Medicine* 1 (January 30, 2006): 59–66.

40. U.S. Department of Health and Human Services, National Center for Health Statistics, Survey on Child Health (Washington, DC: GPO, 1993.)

41. Greg J. Duncan, Martha Hill, and W. Jean Yeung, "Fathers' Activities and Children's Attainments," Paper presented at a conference on father involvement, October 10–11, Washington, D.C., found in: Wade F. Horn and Tom Sylvester, *Father Facts* 4th, www.fatherhood.org.

42. Ibid.

43. Harris Goldstein, "Fathers' absence and cognitive development of 12–17 year-olds," *Psychological Reports* 51 (1982): 843–8.

44. YMCA 200. Strong Families' Survey. Telephone survey conducted December 7–9, 1999, by Global Strategy Group of New York City for the YMCA of the USA.

45. Joseph E. Schwartz et al., "Sociodemographic and psychosocial factors in childhood as predictors of adult mortality," *American Journal of Public Health* 85 (1995): 1237–45.

46. Claudette Wassil-Grimm, *Where's Daddy? How Divorced, Single and Widowed Mothers Can Provide What's Missing When Dad's Missing* (New York: Overlook Press, 1994).

47. Henry Biller, *Fathers and Families: Paternal factors in child development* (Westport, CT: Greenwood Publishing Group, Inc., 1993).

48. R. P. Lederman, W. Chan, and C. Roberts-Gray, "Sexual risk attitudes and intentions of youth aged 12–14 years: Survey comparisons of parent-teen prevention and control groups," *Behavioral Medicine* 29 (2004): 155–63.

49. Lee Smith, "The new welfare of illegitimacy," *Fortune*, April 1994, 81–94.

50. Mark Clemens, *Parade*, February 2, 1997; E. M. Hetherington and B. Martin, "Family Interaction," *Psychopathological Disorders of Childhood* (New York: John Wiley & Sons, 1979): 247–302.

51. Hetherington and Martin, "Family Interaction."

52. Ibid.

53. Barbara Dafoe Whitehead, "Facing the Challenges of Fragmented Families," *Philanthropy Roundtable* 9.1 (1995): 21.

54. N. Zill and Carol Schoenborn, "Child development, learning and emotional problems: Health of our nation's children," U.S. Department of Health and Human Services, National Center for Health Statistics, Advance Data 1990, (Washington, DC: GPO, 1990).

55. Hetherington and Martin, "Family Interaction."

56. Richard Koestner, Carol Franz, and Joel Weinberger, "The family origins of empathic concern: A twenty-six-year longitudinal study," *Journal of Personality and Social Psychology* 58 (1990): 709–17.

57. Wade F. Horn and Tom Sylvester, *Father Facts* (Gaithersburg, MD: National Fatherhood Initiative, 2002).

58. Ibid.

59. C. D. Ryff and M. M. Seltzer, *The Parental Experience in Midlife* (Chicago: University of Chicago Press, 1996).

Chapter Three: You Are Her First Love

1. http://www.medinstitute.org/health/critical_concepts.html?critical_concepts_item=9736&db_item=listitem.

2. Joeanne Gutzwiller, J. M. Oliver, and Barry M. Katz, "Eating Dysfunctions in College Women: The Roles of Depression and Attachment to Fathers," *Journal of American College Health* 52 (1): 27–32.

3. http://www.mayoclinic.com/health/anorexia/DS00606/DSEC-TION=7.

4. L. B. Mintz and N. E. Betz, "Prevalence and Correlates of Eating Disordered Behaviors among Undergraduate Women," *Journal of Counseling and Psychology* 35 (1988): 463–71.

5. R. A. Botta and R. Dumlao, "How Do Conflict and Communication Patterns between Fathers and Daughters Contribute to or Offset Eating Disorders?" *Health Communication 2002*; 14 (2): 199–219.

6. Gutzwiller, Oliver, and Katz, "Eating Dysfunctions in College Women."

7. Ibid.

Chapter Five: Protect Her, Defend Her

1. *With One Voice: America's Adults and Teens Sound Off about Teen Pregnancy—A National Survey* (Washington, DC: The National Campaign to Prevent Teen Pregnancy, April 2001).

2. "Sex on TV 4: Executive Summary 2005," Henry J. Kaiser Foundation Executive Summary, found at: http://www.kff.org/entmedia/upload/Sex-on-TV-4-Executive-Summary.pdf.

3. D. T. Fleming et al., "Herpes Simplex Virus Type 2 in the United States, 1976 to 1994," *New England Journal of Medicine* 337 (1997): 1105–60.

4. J. M. Walboomers et al., "Human Papillomavirus Is a Necessary Cause of Invasive Cervical Cancer Worldwide," *Journal of Pathology* 189 (1999): 12–19.

5. C. M. Roberts, J. R. Pfister, and S. J. Spear, "Increasing Proportion of Herpes Simplex Type 1 as a Cause of Genital Herpes Infection in College Students," *Sexually Transmitted Diseases* 2003 (10): 801–02.

6. Thomas R. Eng and William T. Butler, eds., Committee on Prevention and Control of Sexually Transmitted Diseases, Institute of Medicine, *The Hidden Epidemic: Confronting Sexually Transmitted Disease* (Washington, DC: National Academy Press, 1997).

7. D. N. Fisman, M. Lipsich, E. W. Hook, III, and S. J. Goldie, "Projection of the Future Dimensions and Costs of the Genital Herpes Simplex Type 2 Epidemic in the United States," *Sexually Transmitted Diseases,* October 2002, 29 (10): 608–22.

8. National Center for HIV, STD, and TB Prevention, Centers for Disease Control and Prevention, U.S. Department of Health and Human Services, "Tracking the Hidden Epidemics," www.cdc/gov.com.

9. Ibid.

10. Eng and Butler, *The Hidden Epidemic.*

11. National Center for HIV, STD, and TB Prevention, "Tracking the Hidden Epidemics."

12. Ibid.

13. Walboomers et al., "Human Papillomavirus Is a Necessary Cause of Invasive Cervical Cancer Worldwide."

14. J. Mork et al., "Human Papillomavirus Infection as a Risk Factor for Squamous Cell Carcinoma of the Head and Neck," *New England Journal of Medicine* 15 (2001): 1125–31.

15. Fleming et al., "Herpes Simplex Virus Type 2 in the United States."

16. R. Rector, K. Johnson, L. Noyes, and S. Martin, "The harmful effects of early sexual activity and multiple sexual partners among women: A book of charts," Washington, DC: The Heritage Foundation, 2003. See: http://www.heritage.org/Research/Family/loader.cfm?url=/commonspot/security/getfile.cfm&PageID =44695.

17. Ibid.

18. L. Warner, J. Clay-Warner, J. Boles, and J. Williamson, "Assessing Condom Use Practices: Implications for Evaluating Method and User Effectiveness," *Sexually Transmitted Diseases* 25 (1998): 273–77.

19. National Institute of Allergy and Infectious Diseases, National Institutes of Health, Department of Health and Human Services. "Workshop Summary: Scientific Evidence on Condom Effectiveness for Sexually Transmitted Disease Prevention," July 20, 2001.

20. L. Ku, F. L. Sonenstein, and J. H. Pleck, "The Dynamics of Young Men's Condom Use During and Across Relationships," *Family Planning Perspectives* 26 (1994): 246–51.

21. Denise D. Hallfors, et al, "Which Comes First in Adolescence: Sex and Drugs or Depression?" *American Journal of Preventive Medicine* 29 (2005): 3.

Chapter Seven: Be the Man You Want Her to Marry

1. Thomas Lickona and Matthew Davidson, *Smart & Good High Schools: Integrating Excellence and Ethics for Success in School, Work, and Beyond,* (Cortland, NY: Center for the 4th and 5th Rs (Respect & Responsibility)/ Washington, DC: Character Education Partnership.)

Chapter Eight: Teach Her Who God Is

1. Christian Smith with Melinda Lundquist Denton, *Soul Searching: The Religious and Spiritual Lives of American Teenagers* (New York: Oxford University Press, 2005), 218–64.
2. Ibid., 224.
3. Ibid., 222.
4. Ibid., 151.
5. Ibid., 152.
6. Ibid., 153.
7. Ibid., 151.
8. Ibid., 152.
9. Ibid., 153.
10. Ibid., 151.
11. Ibid., 225.
12. Michael D. Resnick et al., "Protecting Adolescents from Harm: Findings from the National Longitudinal Survey of Adolescent Health," *Journal of the American Medical Association* 278 (1997): 823–32.
13. Smith with Denton, 222.
14. Ibid.
15. Ibid.
16. Ibid., 228.
17. Ibid., 223.
18. Ibid.
19. Ibid., 222.

20. J. W. Sinha et al., "Adolescent Risk Behaviors and Religion: Findings from a National Study," *Journal of Adolescence* (May 3, 2006). Available online at: http://doi:10.1016/j.adolescence.2006.02.005.
21. Smith with Denton, 21.
22. G. W. Comstock and K. B. Partridge, "Church Attendance and Health," *Journal of Chronic Disease* 25 (1972): 665–72.
23. S. Stack et al., "The Effect of the Decline in Institutionalized Religion on Suicide, 1954–1978," *Journal for the Scientific Study of Religion* 22: 239–52.
24. R. L. Gorsuch and D. Aleshire, "Christian Faith and Ethnic Prejudice: A Review and Interpretation of Research," *Journal for the Scientific Study of Religion* 13 (1982): 281–307.
25. Ibid.
26. Ibid.
27. Ibid.
28. Smith with Denton, 30–71.
29. Ibid.
30. Ibid., 260.
31. Centers for Disease Control, *Morbidity and Mortality Weekly Report*, June 9, 2006, 1–108.
32. Armand M. Nicholi, Jr., ed., *The Harvard Guide to Psychiatry* (Cambridge, MA: The Belknap Press of Harvard University Press, 1999), 622–23.
33. A. M. Culp, M. M. Clyman, and R. E. Culp, "Adolescent Depressed Mood, Reports of Suicide Attempts, and Asking for Help," *Adolescence* 30: (1995) 827–37.
34. Jane R. Dickie et al., "Parent-Child Relationships and Children's Images of God," *Journal for the Scientific Study of Religion*, 1997, 36 (1): 25–43.
35. Ibid.
36. Ibid.
37. Smith with Denton, 75.
38. Ibid., 162.
39. Ibid., 27.
40. Ibid., 263.
41. Ibid., 261.

Index

fathers (*continued*)

God, teaching about and, 6, 177–97, 235–36; grit, teaching and, 132–43; as heroes, 6, 29–48; humility, teaching and, 6, 77–92; importance of, 4–5, 7–28, 232–33; leadership of, 4, 30–40; love for daughters of, 3, 5, 7–8; as role models for husbands, 151–75; as moral guides, 34–36, 208–17; parent connectedness and, 219–29; peer pressure and, 48; perseverance of, 40–48; pragmatism of, 123–27, 127–32; protection of daughters by, 3, 6, 93–121, 233–34

feminism, 47, 215

forgiveness, God and, 190

G

genital herpes (herpes simplex type 2), 19, 20, 100, 102, 106, 107

Gerberding, Julie, 108, 109

Giedd, Jay, 55

God: belief in, 180–81; death and, 186, 189; fathers as first image of, 190–93; fear of, 192; forgiveness and, 190; hope and, 85–86, 183–84, 186–90; love of, 83–86; necessity of, 177; teaching about, 6,

177–97, 235–36. *See also* religion

gonorrhea, 100, 106

Graham, Billy, 158

grit: divorce and, 144–45; family and, 133, 136–43, 143–45; problem solving and, 133–35

H

happiness: humility and, 78, 86–88; religion and, 179

HBO, 22

herpes simplex type 1 (cold sores), 100, 107

herpes simplex type 2 (genital herpes), 19, 20, 100, 102, 106, 107, 109, 110

Hilton, Paris, 81

Hispanics, depression and, 21

HIV (human immunodeficiency virus), 9, 12, 97, 109

homosexuality, sex education and, 11, 12

honesty: drug use and, 153–54; fathers as models of good men and, 153–60; humility and, 79; integrity and, 153, 155, 160–64; parent connectedness and, 225–26; pornography and, 153, 154–58

hope: fathers' confidence and, 2; God and, 85–86, 183–84, 186–90

MEG MEEKER, M.D., has spent the past twenty years practicing pediatric and adolescent medicine and counseling teens and parents. Dr. Meeker is a fellow of the American Academy of Pediatrics and a fellow of the National Advisory Board of the Medical Institute. Dr. Meeker is a popular speaker on teen issues and is frequently heard on nationally syndicated radio and television programs. She lives and works in Traverse City, Michigan, where she shares a medical practice with her husband, Walter Meeker. They have four children.

About the Type

This book was set in Sabon, a typeface designed by the well-known German typographer Jan Tschichold (1902–74). Sabon's design is based upon the original letter forms of Claude Garamond and was created specifically to be used for three sources: foundry type for hand composition, Linotype, and Monotype. Tschichold named his typeface for the famous Frankfurt type-founder Jacques Sabon, who died in 1580.